One Man's Music

The Life and Times of Texas Songwriter Vince Bell

by Vince Bell

Number 3 in the North Texas
Lives of Musicians Series

University of North Texas

Denton, Texas

10 9 8 7 6 5 4 3 2 1

Permissions:
University of North Texas Press
1155 Union Circle #311336
Denton, Texas 76203-5017

The paper used in this book meets the minimum requirements of the American National Standard for Permanence of Paper for Printed Library Materials, z39.48.1984. Binding materials have been chosen for durability.

Library of Congress Cataloging-in-Publication Data

Bell, Vince.
   One man's music : the life and times of Texas songwriter Vince Bell / by Vince Bell.
   p. cm.—(North Texas lives of musicians series ; no. 3)
   Includes index.
   ISBN-13: 978-1-57441-266-6 (cloth : alk. paper)
   ISBN-10: 1-57441-266-3 (cloth : alk. paper)
   ISBN-13: 978-1-57441-267-3 (pbk. : alk. paper)
   ISBN-10: 1-57441-267-1 (pbk. : alk. paper)
   1. Bell, Vince. 2. Country musicians—Texas—Biography. 3. Country music—History and criticism. 4. Blues musicians—Texas—Biography. 5. Blues (Music)—History and criticism. I. Title. II. Series.
   ML420.B332A3 2009
   782.421642092—dc22
   [B]

                                                          2008045502

One Man's Music: The Life and Times of Texas Songwriter Vince Bell is Number 3 in the North Texas Lives of Musicians Series.

All Vince Bell songs © Vince Bell. Published by TVB Publishing (BMI), Vince Bell Publishing (SESAC), Bug Music and/or Black Coffee Music. Administered by Bug Music.

Thank you to Gary Burgess for permission to reprint his song: "Frankenstein." Written by Gary Burgess. © Gary Burgess. Administered by Bug Music. Used by permission.

Interior design by Joseph Parenteau.

The dead level best thing I ever did in music
was to find someone to share it with.
This book is dedicated to my wife, Sarah Wrightson

and to my father

This is one man's music and not a history of a time or people nor any other person's story. If there are errors or oversights they are unintentional.

My appreciation and gratitude goes to all the people who helped me bring this to print after a decade of writing, editing, and publishing two separate books, and especially to Karen DeVinney, Dr. Gretchen M. Bataille, and everyone at the University of North Texas Press who inspired me to write my story.

Special thanks go to O'Brien Young for editing and encouraging me to write like who I am, to Kevin Avery for standing with me, and to Wayne and Lisa Lawrence.

Many people gave up endless hours to be interviewed: Lana Bell, Lisa Bell Brasic, Bill Browder, Steven Fromholz, Shary Bell Hammond, Stephen and Franci Jarrard, Tim Leatherwood, Jim McGarry, Mandy Mercier, Larry Monroe, Sam Richardson, Bob Sturtevant, Hobart Taylor, and Kathleen Vick. Thank you for being my memory.

And to Vince Pawless, because we both have many more stories to tell.

Contents

Illustrations

after page 134

1. 1970 practice promo photo.
2. My first promotional poster done in 1971.
3. On KHOU-TV in Houston.
4. At the Old Quarter in Houston.
5. At Anderson Fair with Sandy Mares.
6. Afternoon on the patio at Anderson Fair.
7. Calendar for Anderson Fair.
8. Austin era promo for Moon Hill Management.
9. The poster for the ballet *Bermuda Triangle*.
10. In the cabin on Lake Tahoe.
11. Music School.
12. Portrait by James Minor.
13. Hobart Taylor, Greg Freeman and I while recording the songs for the *Complete Works*.
14. With Nanci Griffith.
15. Recording *Phoenix*.
16. Recording *Phoenix* with Fritz Richmond, Geoff Muldaur and Bob Neuwirth.
17. *Phoenix* cover art as a work-in-progress.
18. At the Paradiso in Amsterdam.
19. With Iain Mathews and Eric Taylor in Zurich.
20. With Mark Olsen.
21. Onstage at the Bottom Line.
22. The last time I saw Townes Van Zandt.
23. Backstage at the Bottom Line with Lyle Lovett, Steven Fromholz, Guy Clark, Willis Alan Ramsey, and Alan Pepper.
24. Lyle, Victor Krauss, and I rehearsing my songs.
25. With Lyle and the band performing.
26. Mainstage at the Kerrville Folk Festival, 2005.

"Young people ask me sometimes, 'Well, Mr. Van Zandt, I would like to do what you do. How do I go about it?' Well, you have to get a guitar or a piano. Guitars are easier to carry. And then you have to blow everything else off. You have to blow off your family. You have to blow off comfort. You have to blow off money. You have to blow off security. You have to blow off your ego. You have to blow off everything except your guitar. Sleep with it, learn how to tune it and no matter how hungry you get, stick with it. You'll be amazed at the amount of people that turns away."

—Townes Van Zandt
From an interview with Margit
Detweiler, 1996

ONE MAN'S MUSIC

One man's music plays
like one man's heart.
There is no giving in
right from the start.

Oh, my love,
one man's music
is my love.

One man's music sings
like one man's song.
Some lead beyond the van,
some string along.

One man's music stands
the weight of time.
Like diamonds in the rough
for one to find.

Foreword

*O*ther music autobiographies give us the culture and history surrounding the artist, the circumstances of his or her life. Vince Bell does this; he also invites us to enter his personal realm of suffering and to attempt to heal along with him, compelling us to look deeply at our own relationship to pain and struggle.

But this is more than a story about a tragic car accident that left Vince in a coma for four weeks. A Foreword presents a few words *before* the body of the book, but it should also let us look *forward* to the book. Vince Bell's story is ultimately uplifting and inspiring, a story of pain, suffering and also hope woven into one rich tapestry that is, indeed, one man's music. We all have songs to sing and stories to tell; Vince Bell invites us into his head to hear his songs and his stories.

Vince Bell is often mentioned along with Townes Van Zandt, Guy Clark, Stevie Ray Vaughan (who was playing with him on his last session before the wreck), Tom Waits, Randy Newman, Eric Clapton, Neil Young and Lucinda Williams, and his songs have been performed and recorded by Little Feat, Lyle Lovett, and Nanci Griffith, and others. And for good reason do these troubadours choose his words to sing. No one can tell this story quite like Vince. He describes scenes that we can see, feel, and smell, such as an icy blast of cold air in a room with Townes Van Zandt. Or the texture of a mouthful of beets that he can't taste because the tasting part of his brain has not yet healed.

Seeing the healing through his eyes and heart gives the reader a chance to understand a man motivated by a rare calling, the pull of his art from death to life. As a student of literature for over 45 years, I see his story in a literary context; we can compare him to Kafka, Rimbaud, Van Zandt and Billy Joe Shaver, all men who had to tell their story as part of their choice to live.

We not only hear Vince's story, but we also read the stories of those around him through interviews. That choice takes us on a full circle around the event. What friends saw happening to him becomes as important as what he felt inside. Vince's essays on life through and around his guitar add another context to this book. Reading the book provides a well-rounded version of one man's life, reminding us that much can be gained from gathering other perspectives on how we live our own life.

Many would give up, when Vince just asked for more opportunities to fail in the hope that one day he would emerge victorious. Now time finds Vince visiting conferences and schools across the country, telling his story in an effort to encourage and educate. This book documents the journey, thus calling us to question our own journey through life. Are we still on the court playing ball as is Vince Bell? Do we value life enough to work this hard? Finishing this book will leave you with your own serious questions to answer. One just might be: "What would I have done?"

Sam Phillips wrote the foreword for my first book on Texas songwriters. That fact alone reminds me of the privilege I have in writing a foreword for Vince's story of his life, his music, his journey. Just as Sam let others know to look forward to my book, so I want you to look forward to all you'll learn in Vince's story.

> Prof. Kathleen Hudson, Director of Texas
> Heritage Music Foundation, author of *Women in
> Texas Music: Stories and Songs* and *Telling Stories,
> Writing Songs: An Album of Texas Songwriters*
> www.kathleenhudson.net
> www.texasheritagemusic.org

♪　𝓘　♪

Sorcerer's Apprentice

𝓘've played music since I was a B-flat cornet-packing kid. I've grown up in music, worked to distraction in music, married unsuccessfully in music, and I've been at it for several wife-times. High musical seasons and adventurous women they were. But even before those delightfully shaped dreadnoughts tacked through my life and always in their wake, there had been only one guitar. It leaned up against a wall or a speaker box and cast ever-blooming, ever-changing melodies from an honored niche in all their houses.

My guitar and I began like a storm in the screened-in second story of a house in the Montrose, an older part of Houston. It was a lawless, hip world-within-the-world, an attitude as much as a place to live, and an anything-goes lifestyle with a soundtrack familiar to everyone in jeans under 30. The musical messages that spoke to us were broadcast from one of several radio stations downtown or on Lovett Boulevard. I was 19 years old when I moved lock, stock, and bicycle into a filthy, roach-infested little flat there. The rest of the city outside the loop dissolved into irrelevance.

The Montrose had seen many a fine day and by the '70s was conveniently overlooked, but it persevered in a discarded kind of way. It was full of rundown two- and three-story brick, stucco, and shiplap houses where the long-haired but balding survivors of the '60s lived. Every kind of human perturbation was partially obscured by a verdant, elephant-eared undergrowth. There was a lot of new paint over a lot of rotten wood. Most of the lawns needed mowing. The roads ran parallel to one another like staves on a sheet of music. Dotting the staves like notes were huge live oak trees. They were stately, ruddy survivors, shading the streets and former avenues. Everything in sight was indelicately in the process of being rained to the ground, but our trendy civilization, powered by the music of the day, blossomed in the cast-aside old town setting.

After we took up residence in that shabby and inexpensive part of town, our lives were gratifying, penniless, illuminating, painful, boring, self-reliant, ill-advised, proud, haphazard, surprising, lucky, heartbreaking, flush, and arduous. We lived our lives off-center in a broken-down but vital part of urban Texas where we couldn't be found if we didn't want to be.

We had everything a young musician with a brand-new guitar could want. We even had our own newspapers and magazines. We lived to get our picture in one, or an article featuring our latest gig. We kept the corner music store in business with all the strings we broke. The local colleges were good for a coffeehouse date from time to time, and the washateria took all the quarters we earned in tips. Night by night we were sorcerers' apprentices. Our robes might have been a little long, but we were casting the first spells of our art in hamburger joints.

There were cool places for us to be seen with our instruments, usually bars, head shops, or late-night eateries among store-fronted fleets of the uncool. We never left a guitar in the car. Better to lose our wallet. That nonsense could be replaced. So we unconditionally hefted the six-string along and slid it below the edge of the table under our feet.

With an address in the Montrose a couple of floors above the street, the cheap Japanese guitar I learned my first chords on and I were at the center of the known universe. We had a backstage pass to a solar system that seemed to revolve around us. The mean age of everyone I would meet in a day was 22, and the gas was 19.9 cents a gallon. I can remember that walking to a different post office a few blocks over from my apartment at Fairview and Van Buren seemed like being in a movie with subtitles. So we never left the neighborhood more often than required.

♪   *II*   ♪

Look of the Loner
Looking at It

*I*n those days I was relentless in my pursuit of a resounding, large-bodied guitar like those I had seen that were known as dreadnoughts because of their shape. There were several capable brands, but the one for me was made by the C. F. Martin Company. I looked in all of the big cities within a day's drive: New Orleans, Dallas, Fort Worth, Austin, and San Antonio. Come full circle, I saw the one I would have given the world for at a music store in downtown Houston. It had a defiantly darkish top, unlike the other pallid, almost white spruce-tops I had seen in a year's worth of hunting. It cost as much as you could pay for a guitar of that style, and had come to the bayou town from another store as flood damage from a Corpus Christi hurricane. It simply had the look of the loner who was looking at it.

Hard to play because the strings were unusually high over the fret board, it was typically unforgiving. That feature made you strong. The feel of the instrument's neck was balky compared to other brands, and it was bigger than Texas in the low end. But it was a tempo machine: you could generate the rhythm of a saw or a drum. It would play music, too.

To play acoustic music in that uncomfortably warm, semitropical city you went to a little coffeehouse called Sand Mountain on Richmond Avenue, or to the Old Quarter in downdamntown. If you wanted to stand under the corny red light and play, you had to play at those places.

Most everyone I saw performed with this particular brand of guitar, shapely cousins of the dreadnought I so coveted. A 1968 Martin D-28 dreadnought acoustic guitar. The dark one that had the look of the loner.

The guitar you owned and played was a symbol of your vision. It bestowed a kind of identity among us musicians and writers. With your strings in hand, it was as if you belonged in that arty, dilapidated part of Texas. You strapped them proudly, imposingly, daringly on your hip like a large-caliber revolver. Just like a tousle-haired artist smelling of paint thinner with gracefully fluted brushes like an arrangement of flowers in his back pocket, or a writer with a busy lapel of ball-point pens and a thick, dog-eared journal in his satchel. You could rest assured, if you couldn't be recognized in a carping musical crowd for your tuneful genius, your guitar surely could.

From the very start, I didn't want to play other people's songs as much as I wanted to write them myself. The acoustic guitar was a necessity. It was like having an orchestra hung around your neck. Creating just the right notes where the lyric was the important part could so energize the message. Most of my performances over the next 30 years were with that same guitar. I stood behind it at most every gig since around the time the first NASA astronaut walked on the moon. It introduced me and my compositions up and down a crazy line on a road map starting in the shadow of that dank, tempestuous Texas city and at length winding from San Francisco, California, to Vienna, Austria.

There was some living between the two of us. Sometimes we were like conquering heroes, sometimes like a couple of friendless thieves stealing away in the night. It was a rewarding relationship, as close as my skin, that I developed with a "piece of wood and steel," as my friend Richard Dobson called it.

Early on, I knocked the wind clear out of the guitar like an accordion when I fell belly-down on it. I was being Elvis's little brother in front of an oval garage-sale mirror. The phone rang in my $75-a-month apartment while I was practicing a nervous-kneed but windy stance. I cut my eyes across my shoulder in a back-and-forth staccato to my cloudy likeness. It was all in time with the cadences I played. While hurriedly climbing up a couple of stairs that led to the telephone in the hallway, I tripped with the guitar strapped around my neck. The sound was sickening as I fell flat on the instrument.

As I lay on the floor with the guitar underneath me, the phone stopped ringing. I carefully rolled over like a grieving lover, sat up, and squeezed my eyes shut for a split second. In shock when I opened them wide, I saw that the guitar's side and back had seven cracks. Seven cracks? Emergency lights and sirens whined in my head. I tuned the strings down in fast motion, set the guitar on a pillow, and searched out someone in the phonebook who could look at it. I was at Mr. Gestantes's violin shop at light speed and put the poor instrument lying broken as hell up on the counter. The old man eyed it up and down through a pair of tarnished, wire-rimmed bifocals.

Past the point of being unglued, I managed, "Well, is there anything you can do, sir? Is it as bad as it looks? I-I just can't believe this."

Mr. Gestantes looked a little annoyed, and eyeing me over those thick glasses said, "Settle down, boy. You just re-sculpted it a little bit. Leave it with me. You can pick it up in the morning. Now go on," as he began to lose interest. "I got work to do."

In the end, he didn't even glue the cracks that ran for half a foot along the grain of the bottom. Dismissing me entirely when I came to pick it up, he said, "Doesn't need it. It'll be fine."

He charged me a couple of bucks for my tirade as I laid the spruce top in the cardboard case as if it were the body of that lover. The guitar and I returned to the apartment in a light rain. I resumed rehearsing the stance and the tunes.

A few years later, the guitar and I lived rent-free in Houston, in a tent in my keyboard player Dan Earhart's yard, maybe 15 blocks from my long-ago upstairs apartment where the music began. We called it "the wildlife refuge." It was the right price and it had location, location, location. You could find me, a blue dog, a chaise lounge, and a typewriter in a green army tent there on several undeveloped acres. There were abandoned culverts around the property and large live oak shade trees throughout. And like the rest of that part of town, no one ever mowed the lawn.

Because of the phalanxes of blood-crazed mosquitoes I slathered down with DEET. At night the flashlight attracted them by the zillions. The only thing between me and a drone of uncountable insects was the glowing, thin skin of that surplus-store tent.

The backyard abutted the unfenced, overgrown space. Sometimes it rained so hard and got so deep so fast that Dan would take pity on us and let the dog and me come indoors to dry out some. When the rain came down the hardest, he would always have an espresso pot of Bustello just beginning to boil and a tray of some beat Mexican pot. Coffee and marijuana: drug maintenance and the first two things you needed to start a rock 'n' roll band, even ahead of a new set of strings.

The monsoon lasted most all year, so the guitar was always in his front room way before us. Life was funky in flippers.

The wheels kept turning while my fingertips drummed out movements of another three-minute wonder on a long, green Samsonite-looking counter-top covered with salt and pepper shakers. There were breakfasts in varying states of completion and paper-napkin dispensers. I was balancing on a barstool in a Houston diner. It was late, and I was hauling that 28 I had played to maybe six people. All night. And I think all six were now here in the diner.

Another cup of coffee, a quarter for the service, and I paced around the local warp in space/time poking at numbers and letters on the jukebox. I wrapped the gray wool muffler around my neck again. It was cold in the Calcutta of the western hemisphere.

The cook was gay, worked the late-night shift, and pierced people's ears on the side. Eric Taylor dared me, so I gave "Cookie" 15 bucks and he popped me in the left ear with a little machine that looked like a pop gun without the stock. So much for my chili size. I began to warp like cardboard. The neon-lit room became a director's cut of *Twilight Zone* with the short-order cook, the waitress, six kooky-looking types, Eric, and me in it.

I punch-drunkenly stumbled into the night slung to that guitar like it was a shield, the spanking stud of gold burning in my left lobe. From the driver's seat of my vomit-green Rambler American I tossed the chili-size doggy bag in a dumpster. The next day nobody noticed my earring.

Left Wichita Falls after a gig at a little club run by Jim Richey that was the former restaurant to a quiet '50s motel owned by a family of Pakistanis. It was called the Flamingo. We musicians called it the Flaming O. Most of us played it every couple of months. Didn't much have to bother writing this one down in the date book. It was on the itinerary for a flock of Austin-to-Dallas acts for a while. Like today, some great opportunities to hear Texas music were sometimes up in Tornado Alley along the Oklahoma border.

I left the next morning late after a night that had lasted till damn well dawn. I was in a hurry to do something 250 miles away. There were cops all along this route, and I was severely compromised from the vat of beer I had wallowed in the night before. In other words, I was rather crispy around the edges and probably more worried about dying than getting pulled over. I'd gone almost 40 miles and it was already blinding and hot as blazes on that two-lane back to Fort Worth.

I hunched down over the steering wheel in "The Rock 'n' Roll Hotel," my white Chevy utility van. The windows were down, the vent was open full blast, and my hair was blowing under the pith helmet I wore. Out from under a pair of sunglasses, I sweated in a 60-mile-an-hour wind until I looked in the rearview mirror into the flatbed behind my seat. There was a pile of guitar stands, the tire iron, a can of 30-weight rolling around, mic cords, a clothes bag, and a spare tire. But wait just one minute, that guitar in its case was not infuckingcredibly there.

I had done some pretty out-there things in the past, and apparently I wasn't through yet. But this one stung all the way back to the joint in that stifling, overpowering heat. Forty retraced miles later there was the damned guitar waiting for me, right where I had left it, behind the stage at the Flaming O. I drove at light speed all the way back to where I was when the light had come on. Then I could kick one foot up on the dash and settle back into being in a hurry about something I couldn't recall.

That six-string and I outlived the most opulent clubs, the most hole-in-the-wall dives, and generations of listeners in the message-hungry towns of the world. Beginning in 1971, we played our musical style to an ever-deepening cadre of people. We often arrived and left alone. Hot, humid, lovelorn, hungover? Roll down the window. The privilege of surviving yesterdays too many to count is to see that both that great, big-sounding guitar and I are still talking to each other.

Sweat Like a Boxer

*T*he Old Quarter was a rundown, two-story stucco-over-brick blockhouse of a building with iron bars across broken, cloudy windows. If you played in Houston, this was the gig everyone wanted. The entrance was ten-foot-high barn doors that could not be locked without a chain and a stout two-by-four. They hung below a rusting, wrought-iron signboard swinging in the sticky humidity from the Gulf of Mexico.

The joint on the forgotten corner of Austin and Congress streets looked like an abandoned building. It was within earshot of the nightly howling that issued from behind the bars of the Harris County Jail for Women. Across a block of broken cement making a patchwork wasteland of parking lots was what you would certainly call several floors of America's most pissed-off gentlewomen.

Dale Sofar, one of the owners of the Old Quarter, drove a Jeep to the club every night with a pooch named Pup next to him and a keg of beer in the back. With a water bowl behind the bar, the little dog confidently roamed the block around the club like a policeman taking names. Inside, the dog would promenade on top of the bar before falling asleep in the middle of our sets. Ownership of this four-footed lady-killer seemed a touch murky between Dale and the other owner, Wrecks Bell. Wrecks lived upstairs in a room with nothing but a mattress on the floor, a bass guitar without a case in the corner, Lightnin' Hopkins records everywhere, and a water bowl for Pup.

Like the dog, I was there every evening, gig or no, hauling spent kegs or stacking boxes of empty beer bottles for Joy Llewellan and Jan Holly, the young ladies who bartended. When they didn't have busywork I'd still be there, playing pool for money on a quarter table. More often than not, I made more money shaking down the permapressed tourists who unwisely challenged me to a game of nine-ball than I did downstairs playing for the cover charge.

But play I would. Most any night of the week. The problem back then was that not many wanted to hazard into the old part of town to watch a kid learn how perform his own songs, regardless of how hip and cool it was.

One night I teed it up for a skeleton crew of an audience, maybe eight people. In the front row there were a couple of collegiate-looking types. A blonde girl, but not too blonde, and a tall guy, but not too tall, sat there squeaky clean. They were so suburban they glowed.

In front of them on a pedal-sewing-machine frame converted into a bar table sat a large birthday cake with lots of green icing. As I completed the first low-key, downtown, 45-minute set of the night, the couple giggled and complimented me on the wonderful music.

The disarming young girl said, "It's Buster's birthday. You've made it so nice with your music, we want you to have a piece of his birthday cake."

So I said, "Sure. And thanks."

She replied, "Have a lot of the green icing. I made it myself."

Ten minutes later I heard a buzzing in my ear. After a short while, I realized it wasn't going away anytime soon. I looked around the bar, and our youthful couple had made the rounds of the place, giving large pieces of that cake to everyone who was interested, including one of the owners.

When I belatedly began the next set, I felt like I was in an elevator going up. I looked down in front and the young couple, back in place with a large empty cake pan, could have been posing for a horror movie. I looked at them as squarely as I could under the circumstances and said, "You didn't, did you?"

They nodded up and down slowly, as if in a trance. They were demoniacally smiling but their faces weren't moving. They had put LSD in the green icing. After the shock wore off that the entire bar had been stoned by a couple of kids from West Houston, the rest of that night the jukebox played the tunes and the beer was free from a bartender seemingly without a care in the world. I didn't make much in tips, but I guess I didn't work that hard, either. I sure smiled a lot before I came down the next day.

Thirty years later I pulled up in a windy parking lot just off the Strand in Galveston, Texas. After leashing the dog to my arm, I walked into . . . the Old Quarter, with Wrecks Bell behind the bar. No pool table here, but, just like the original club back in Houston, the dartboard on the wall above an old sofa, made of some faded and fraying petroleum product, was as familiar as a recurring dream.

After a thousand roadhouse nights in a dozen countries on two continents, I asked somewhat self-consciously, "Can I bring my dog in here?" Wrecks rolled his eyes, "This is the *Old* Quarter, man," as he popped the top off a cold Texas beer and handed me the water bowl for the dog.

My border collie fell asleep on the floor that night just like Pup had on the bar. I played the hours away to familiar attention from a roomful of people who had probably seen me first at the old Old Quarter.

I shut my eyes ever tighter while singing some of the same old songs, on the same old guitar, that I had performed there decades ago.

Perhaps it's true, I thought in the middle of one of them, that some of the dearest things really do not change.

Many of us Houston kids of the '70s grew up at the Old Quarter while learning to pinch the poetry just so, loving and hating, fighting and embracing, and every one of us sweating the shirts to our backs. I used to hate to play the opening sets because the sun wouldn't even be down at that time. You sweat like a boxer by the end of one set of songs.

♪ *IV* ♪

Sinbad and the Silver Tooth

*I*t was Friday night and the witching hour was at hand. Townes Van Zandt was going to play at the Old Quarter. I put on my singer's uniform of anything-other-than-cowboy boots, tight-fitting jeans, and a working-class white shirt under a sports coat of some righteous non-color. And, of course, I packed along my bronze-string "cannon" 28 like an outsized ID card.

Townes was originally from Houston, and I had known him from other clubs. He was now living in Nashville, which made him extra famous at home, and everyone was buzzing about his return for this gig. The last time he teed it up at the OQ, he had recorded a double-set album of his immortals that turned up in everyone's record collection sooner or later. All my songwriter friends would be there. Now that I was sufficiently suited up, I was going to be there, too. I admired this man for displaying character in his simple but elevating work. I intended to embody the same in mine.

The Old Quarter was packed. I arrived just as Dale, the tall, slender, and tanned fellow who resembled a good-looking Groucho Marx, was making the introduction from a booking calendar in his hand. He was calm as he spoke and he smiled a lot. The large crowd was settled more and more by his every comment and gesture. He was like the host of a variety show. No one could work a crowd better, including most of us who played his club. By the time the background music stopped, you could hear a pin drop.

At the same time, Townes climbed somewhat unsteadily down a flight of stairs from the upstairs back room. He sat off to the side of the barroom absorbing yet another brew to chase the whiskey in his other hand. His broad smile exposed a silver tooth that made him look reachable, like he knew something you very well might want to know. But his eyes stayed at half-mast and unimpressed, like he was sure not going to tell. Alcohol does funny things to people. He was the loudest thing in the room during his long introduction as he boisterously chuckled with the woman tending bar. The guitar hung loosely from his shoulder like a rifle. It swung around precariously as he swilled another shot straight from the black-labeled bottle and tipsily poured one for the bartender.

"Good to see your smiling faces, people. That's the schedule for who's going to play here in the next month," presided Dale. "Now help me out and put your hands together for a great friend of mine and the only songwriter we could find on such short notice."

The place erupted in an accolade. Just as quickly as it heated up, however, it settled down. We were all intent on every word for the better part of the introduction to the first song. But something was amiss deluxe. The first piece was a familiar song the crowd had been listening to for their musical lifetimes. They probably all owned the record that it appeared on. It was easy to suppose they could have sung it themselves. Some tried to that night, as if to help Townes to the recollection. He began that number, but before he finished a couplet of the verse, he stopped. Then he laughed and tried to regain momentum. Starting it all up again, jerkily stopping, and just as jerkily starting and stopping again.

"No really, lemme start over. Aw, lemme try another one." To no avail. And when Townes realized that he just could not pull it off, he sat up straighter and tried to tell a joke that he could not remember the punch line to. He probably attempted the same tune ten times before he went grousing about for another. The black-labeled bottle was in charge now.

People didn't take long before they were making for the door. This wasn't the first time this local legend had pulled a swan dive. The poor fellow miscued almost all the chords and almost all the words. It didn't seem he could make that many miscues in between the passages he simply forgot. There was practically a rush to get out of the place.

Townes had dumbfounded himself by now. And you could no longer see the offhand, jocular glint of the silver tooth. It just wasn't funny anymore. For three sets that night he unsuccessfully attempted to finish a single song. Toward the end of the second set I couldn't watch anymore and went upstairs and won money on the quarter pool table. Probably got a little drunk myself.

I was flipped. I wouldn't leave, but I was flipped. All us young songwriters looked up to Townes. He had always shown us how far the creatively simple could go, that songs could be as revealing as a good piece of literature. His were songs for the songwriters. And this was what we all worked our fannies off for, the right to tell the story ingeniously, clearly, and in our own words. I wanted to feel sorry for him, but I was hard in an ignorant kind of way like someone who had no idea of his trials. I just knew he wasn't doing what I wanted him to do. But I knew the rules, too, and lived by them myself. This was an uncomfortable lesson in what not to do.

After a while, I tired of taking friends' money. The show was over. The room downstairs was now empty and dark. Where there had been loyal legions of diehard fans, now there was only a cold, unfulfilled vacancy. After climbing down those uneven stairs, I sat down next to the still drunk but obviously dejected singer as people cleaned up the bar for tomorrow night's show.

I offered, "Tough one tonight, eh, amigo?"

He thickly intoned under his breath, "No one to blame but me. But shit [hiccup], I don't care. I've played this place a thousand times drunker than that [hiccup]. Listen, if you gimme a ride to this fancy downtown high-rise I'm staying at, I got some alcohol there. I'll get you drunk if you gimme a ride."

I couldn't see how I could turn him down. Hell, I wouldn't. I'd been brought up with the rumors about this colorful fellow. I guess I just wanted to be part of a rumor myself. It made me feel a little taller somehow to consider it. Be careful what you wish for.

Back then the opening act (that's me) was a lower life-form to the headliner (that was him). He was the famous writer, and I was just one of the new kids with a lot of ink in my pen who had modeled a few of my own early compositions after his. Before he moved to that country-and-western town, he once taught me how to play an A-minor chord in the back room of Sand Mountain Coffeehouse. I always loved the sound of an Am chord after that. Townes was a gracious fellow to have bothered with a hardheaded youngster like me. The difference between us was that he performed for packed houses, while I once defiantly nailed the quarter I made in the tip jar to the wall behind the stage.

So there we were finishing the last beers of the evening together. We toasted on the last drop and packed our guitars for the door. It was like I belonged, and I was thrilled to lead him right out the door into that windy, freezing midnight.

A frigid gale blasted me in the face. My station wagon was just a few steps away. As I keyed the tailgate door Townes broke off down the sidewalk into the cutting wind. "Whoa, wait a minute pal, my car's over here." He put his guitar down and stumbled farther over to a narrow alley between the brick buildings. He began talking to no one I could discern as he struggled to reach for something between the buildings.

I could hear Townes entreating, "C'mon now. Don't be difficult. It's cat-killing cold out here tonight."

As I approached, he blurted, "Help me get ol' Sinbad out of here. It's too cold." I was stunned but obliged. Townes pulled a wino by the collar out from between the buildings.

"Listen, if you help me get Sinbad to the downtown high-rise I'll get you drunk." I couldn't think anymore. I was truly puzzled. The bizarre evening and now this.

"What the hell, get him in the backseat," I said, as I put both guitars in the rear of the wagon and closed it up. I was willing to pay any price to hang out with this songwriter. He crammed the oblivious fellow into the backseat and hurried into the front himself. I flew behind the wheel and turned the big V-8 over while turning the heater blower to high.

Then, while we made the block and headed uptown, the biggest surprise so far. "Damn, it smells. What the hell is that?"

The pitiful looking, frozen old alcoholic in a filthy metallic-green business suit had been defecating on himself for days in that alley. "Roll the windows down quick," I commanded. We virtually flew down the street going as fast as we could to outrun the awful smell from the backseat. The wind at 35 miles an hour froze us to the bone. At every corner there was a stoplight. And at every stoplight we held our breath. We could only hope the light would change before we ran out of breath.

We arrived at the swank high-rise parking lot. Townes drunkenly grabbed the old man and made for an elevator that would take them both to the sixth floor. I pulled into a space for my car and, though it was freezing cold, I rolled all the windows down to air the place out.

I then took the same elevator up with both of our guitars. The olfactory record of their passage was everywhere. I tried to avoid the overpowering stares of everyone who shared the ride with me.

Ding-ding, sixth floor. I exited like a shot and exhaled when I reached the end of the hall. I knocked on the apartment door. And distantly from inside, "C'mon in, make yourself at home."

"Right," my ass. I threw the instruments and my coat on a crushed velvet couch with claw feet and gold fringe a foot long.

My fingers began to get feeling back in them once more. I was going to find that hooch and thaw out the rest of me now. All I could see was a bottle of vodka and a half empty can of Dr. Pepper on top of the white French bureau in the resplendent apartment. The drawer handles were ornate brass affairs so large you could open a beer bottle with them.

Townes was behind the partly opened bathroom door on one knee. Steam billowed from the door. He had the dumbfounded old man in the Jacuzzi tub. His rancid clothes were already in a grocery bag on the floor. I crumpled the top closed for good measure.

"So, is this all you got? Vodka and Dr. Pepper?"

Then from the bathroom, "Hey man, do you see that sliding glass door to the patio?" I looked out the glass at the festooned buildings of downtown in the blisteringly cold winter wind.

"Yeah, I'm at the door now." I wasn't confused anymore, but I was still tipsy from the beer I had soaked up playing nine-ball. Would that I could have summoned some sober judgment about now.

"Well, go out on the patio and bring me one of those folding chairs around the glass table. Do you see it?"

"Yeah, yeah, I see it. Just a minute." I opened the sliding door just wide enough to slip sideways out onto the arctic patio. I began to put one of the festive, summery-looking chairs under my arm when SLAM! goes the glass door behind me. And there was Townes weaving back and forth, locking the mechanism with a mischievous smile. I was truly fucked.

"Wait a minute, man," my eyes widened in fear. "It's FREEZING out here," I pleaded as he weaved back to the bathroom to the naked, dripping old-timer standing in the tub. My entreaties were to no avail. And there I stood with no cover, six floors up the side of a building at night in a subzero wind chill. I folded out the chair and sat down, resigned to my fate.

Meanwhile, Townes threw a sumptuous-looking towel around the poor old devil, which made things a little better to look at, at least for him. Then, like a hospital nurse, he helped the almost incapacitated man out of the tub, across the bedroom, and slid him between the shimmering silk sheets on the king-size bed. The man's eyes were bulging out from under the bedding like a cartoon character's. His head rested on a monogrammed pillow bigger than he was. He was bright-eyed now and talking some unintelligible wino gibberish at a hundred miles an hour.

Muffled behind the glass but smiling from behind that silver tooth again, Townes consoled, "Now, now. Take it easy. You're gonna bust a gut. Do you see that obnoxious kid out there? On the patio. Yeah, that frosty one. Do you think he's learned his lesson yet? Do you think we should let him in?" The wide-eyed bum was speechless but staring right at me.

I thought, Thanks a lot, old man.

I turned back to the beautiful but demoralizing glacial cityscape. A moment later Townes came around to the sliding door and flipped the lock open. And I was out of that chair and back indoors. As I shivered and shook on the end of the bed, the wino lay transfixed, staring at the chandelier on the bordered ceiling. Townes sauntered over to the chest of drawers, drying his hands on the towel, then screwed open the bottle of vodka over a couple of plastic coffee cups.

"How 'bout a drink, amigo?" one eyebrow higher than the other.

Shaking my head, I did believe I was thirsty. "Make it a double, no ice, and go easy on the Dr. Pepper, thanks."

♪   ✔   ♪

Music Where the Words
Are the Important Part

*O*n many a lonely road to nowhere but my next gig, my instrument set me apart from the mainstream. It rang with an identity in sound that was distinct from any other guitar. It's fair to note that most of this distinction existed only between my ears. My first few lessons about the ragtag of showbiz taught me that if you couldn't fool yourself first, that if an idea didn't light you up like Times Square, you couldn't fool anyone else into believing they were on Times Square. That guitar and I were growing up in a showbiz life together. I was a hopeless kid in an art world that delighted in its own shadow. My saving grace was that I was young and tough enough to be a pain for one loudshoutingwhile.

But I got tired of playing in between songs on the jukeboxes in the same hick towns. Not very far into it yet, I was bored. I even grew weary of well-intentioned folk clubs. I didn't write folk music, and I didn't think folk music. It wasn't my music, my statement. But more often than not, my best efforts to write currently applicable themes were mistakenly referred to as folk music simply because I chose to compose and play with the acoustic guitar.

Folk music was from an impoverished but proud era that I barely understood. It was a WPA thing back in the 1930s, populist and status quo. By the 1970s its message and the way it was performed had degenerated into the traditional.

The words and music I wrote had nothing to do with the traditional. They were as brand new as my naive but developing thoughts could make them. If I lagged in accepting some of the world and its music, the world lagged in its understanding of me, my messages, and how I chose to put them. I was growing up in a brave new setting with perspectives of its own. Although they were far from me at the time, I was working on my own traditions.

John Lennon's writings had been coming together in my thoughts since I was a kid. By the time I started living on my own and trekking outside the Montrose, his tunes blew me through the wall. It didn't hurt one bit that Lennon also played a guitar similar to mine. In three verses and a refrain, he retired a generation or two of the finest poets, as far as I was concerned. He wrote unflinchingly on themes and topics that had nothing to do with the tired old traditions, and he approached the tired old traditions in novel ways. He was in the forefront of a group that presented music different from, but solidly based in, country, blues, and rock 'n' roll. I would love and learn from the music of many others in the mixed bag of musical styles that were the '60s and '70s, but Lennon was, for sure, the first.

He wrote a bold poetry. His words and music seemed to convey the same message. He was someone who could spin a tale with as much attention to what the piece said as to how it sounded. The music amplified the lyric. I had always been into the well-written verse. Lennon recast the treatment of music, and he recast the relationship of lyric to music.

The Beatles albums were hip, beautiful, and moving, every cut. And they rocked. But no duckwalking here. Instead they used those conventions, and several others, to create an interpretation like no other before them. Their music even showcased other music, other arrangements, other instruments. The Beatles brought an intellectually powerful perspective that just hadn't existed before they arrived on the music scene.

A later phenomenon of popular music and an acoustic player himself, Bruce Springsteen, said it well with the line in "No Surrender": "We learned more from a three-minute record than we ever learned in school."

I wanted to write like Lennon but be even more lyrically involved and illuminating. I wanted my music to include the diversity of sophisticated arrangement that his used to accent his lyrics.

While I was learning some of his work and playing my first gigs in Texas, I laid down my last hundred dollars for a plane ticket to New York City and the Bitter End club in Greenwich Village to do one of my first auditions. No guts, no bucks. From that rather bold little wager I found myself performing on the National Coffeehouse Circuit in Idaho, and Colorado, in the mountains to Minnesota, the Dakotas, and Wisconsin. And ultimately back in New Mexico and Texas. There I was scoring gigs at folk clubs with Beatle's songs, a smattering of other pop tunes, and my own early work. Music where the words are the important part.

I'm Not This Way Because I'm a Musician, I'm a Musician Because I'm This Way

*T*he "circuit" began for me in Twin Falls, Idaho. The plane ride felt luxurious compared to driving my Rambler to all the whistle-stops I could lie my way into in the Lone Star State. After we landed, the pilot came over the intercom and advised us that ours was the last plane before a snowstorm and the arrival of the then Vice President. He announced that none of us paying customers would be allowed to enter the terminal.

Employees of the airline and Secret Service goons hurried us through the deplaning. As I was shoved down the walkway from the 727 into the swirling snow, I looked over to the baggage-claim area. There was my precious $500 guitar in its new case, lying in a bank of snow. As I retrieved it and brushed it off, in stormed a baby-blue vice-presidential version of Air Force One. I grabbed my hat as flurries of white obscured us all. The big airliner raced past us.

I looked down at the fancy, alligator-linen-covered hard-shell case I had bought for my guitar and noticed that all the shiny gold grommets on one side were gone, after only one plane ride. That was the most expensive and toughest case you could buy for a guitar, short of an Anvil case. Several more of my cases would be destroyed in years to come in the same manner. I've owned many that came to no good because of baggage monkeys at an airport.

That was just the beginning of what was in store for me on the storied musical road that led over the ever-retreating horizon.

After completing an exhausting tour of colleges in three or four states, this time driving in that Rambler and on the way south homeward, I stopped in Iowa for gas. I had been running on fumes for an hour. Finally I came across a filling station and pulled over in a driving rain. It was lonesome-looking and run-down, but the car was so alarmingly out of gas that anything would do. I jumped out and made for the office and out of the deluge. The windows of the station were cracked, dirty, and fogged up. The advertisements on the walls were ancient and oddly out of step with a cold, drizzly day. They were sun-faded.

After I closed the door behind me the conversation in the room stopped cold as I stood dripping in front of four or five locals. They were eyeing me skeptically up and down, crowded around a wood-burning stove against the back wall.

I exhaled with no small amount of relief, "Not much gas on this route."

"And there's not much here, either," chimed one of the clever fellows.

"Pardon?" I pursed my lips, pulled my stomach in, and put my hands on my hips. "You're kidding?"

No one was laughing, and I could feel their contempt for my long hair and blue-jeaned looks. That's the way it was in those days. "I guess I'll just get a Coke and move on down the road." I walked up to an ancient pop machine, searching in a half-soaked pocket.

Before I could come up with enough change, "There ain't no Cokes, either," another good old boy sneered. 'Nuff said. I never left anyplace so pissed. I couldn't even feel the chill of the rain as it drenched me while I checked the oil with the dipstick.

It was a pure wonder that my car, pulling a homemade wooden trailer full of PA equipment and amplifiers, made it another 12 miles to the next broken-down-looking gas stop in the midst of a cornfield I was driving through that lasted for a day. As I finally filled the tank up, I thought totally unholy thoughts about what those creeps had done to me and what I would like to do to them if they were ever in my neighborhood.

I simmered under my breath, "Come on down to my block, boys."

Sometime in the next year's worth of dates at the colleges, I woke up foggy-headed on a Greyhound bus heading to Valley City, North Dakota. As far as my tired eyes could see I was on a flat, wind-whipped, featureless landscape with nothing much on it except the exit off the interstate. The road wound down into a crease in the Dakota plains. At the bottom of the indention in the earth was my gig and my motel.

I checked in, tuned up, and, a couple of chords into a song I was trying to write, I broke a string. I went looking for a replacement in that Dakota town at the only music store in the county. The owner took one look at my bronze-wound strings and admitted that he could only outfit me with electric guitar nickel flat-wounds. I took the largest gauge I could find. They kind of resembled fence wire without the rust. They sounded and played like the rubber bands from a bunch of broccoli.

When I showed up with my elastic fence wire strung up, the chairman of the coffeehouse committee said, "Gimme a minute, we have to set up for you." I followed him to a sterile-smelling room with a group of students watching a sitcom on a huge console television. It was the only thing in the room other than a couple of sofas and chairs, and was on a raised platform. The chairman and a group of helpers proceeded to pull the plug and clamorously engineered the television to the floor. That caused great dissatisfaction among the students. When they hung three small floodlights in a cardboard box from the ceiling (the light system, I presumed), more grunts from the now almost nonexistent crowd.

By the time the chairman had turned off the room lights and set up a mic stand where the TV used to be, it was just me and that guitar playing for the coffeehouse committee members and the chairman. He left to teach a night class by my third song. I never let on that the poor 28 made my efforts sound like a train derailment, and the audience never knew.

I saw the Panhandle of Texas at a Baptist college playing their coffeehouse. Instead of a motel for my accommodation, I was bivouacked in a spare room in the basement next to the dorm mother. She was a pleasant enough old woman who had one eye that stared you straight in the face. The other eye pointed with an odd sort of virtue to the heavens. She would wake me every morning with a knock like a drill sergeant on my door. When I answered in a haze and a pair of gym shorts, she would sermon, "You know you're wayward, don't you?"

"Yes ma'am, good morning—and good night," as I politely closed the door and went back to bed.

I spent three days there playing ping-pong with the women's basketball team during the afternoons. I did my show at night in the same room. These students introduced themselves to me as the "Queen Bees." They were the number-one women's basketball team in the nation that year, and they acted like it with those paddles, like riot clubs, in their hands. When I won a game from one of them, they circled the table like a pack of hungry hyenas.

After that every one of them wanted a piece of yours truly. Every time I won a point at least one of them would thwack the green-plastic-covered chairs in exasperation. A win on the table against an outlander like me was a badge of some kind to them. High-top tennis shoes and wind sprints, I recalled them from my own kid-hood.

Plainview was also my introduction to the "dry" county. One of the good folks who attended my shows at night told me about alcohol in this small town. "There ain't any," he explained. "You have to go up the highway to Tulia, or down to Floydada. But I'll tell ya where the locals get hooch on the sly." Then with his hands cupped over my ear, "From the night clerk at the hotel down on the town square. By the way, I wasn't going to come out tonight. But I watched you beat that point guard at the table today. So I figured you deserved the cover charge."

Completing my third set of the night at 78 rpms, including some Lennon and some Dylan, I made a beeline to the hotel on the sleepy square. Hell, the whole block around looked abandoned even in the broad daylight. Dry as a bone with a pocketful of money, I walked into the deserted foyer and found one good fellow reading the local paper behind the register. Out of the side of my mouth, "I'd like to buy a six-pack of beer."

"Oh y'would, would'ja?" he returned. "Take a seat. Ah'll be back."

So I sat, and sat, and sat, and noticed a police car drive by intermittently. Well, it wasn't much of a police car, an early '60s model Chevrolet Bel-Air. I'll bet it didn't have any more pickup than my Rambler. The lights on the roof looked like they had been made in someone's garage. They were smallish and the blue wasn't so blue. The red was different shades of orange. The ancient officer of the law behind the wheel had obviously been driving that night shift on the square for a generation or two, I figured. I was thirsty enough that I felt like I could outrun the cop and his machine on foot.

Maybe a full half hour later the man behind the register returned with a paper bag under his arm. "Sorry fer the wait. But ah gotta keep an eye own Mr. Bean. Ah down't thank anyone in this town has the heart tuh retare thet ol' burd. Heh, if anythang happened in'a city limits he'd probably have a hara'tack. D'jounotice? He made those cherry-tops in his shop. Pritty good, huh? This'll duit," he shoved a brown grocery sack to me like it was a bomb. Then he went back to his newspaper as if I wasn't ever there.

I slapped a ten dollar bill down on the check-in desk and split that square with my ill-gotten libations. Timed my getaway to happen between rounds of the antique Chevy with the bald tires. Finished off those six bottles watching the original *Star Trek* on a black-and-white television set back at the dorm.

I tried not to burp too awfully loud so I wouldn't wake the cock-eyed Baptist woman next door.

After each foray into America on the coffeehouse circuit, I came back to play the same old Tejas haunts and a flock of new ones that came into being while I was away from the Gulf Coast. The only thing that had a shorter lifespan than a rock 'n' roll band was a bar. So when I showed up again, my old hangouts were full of new faces. Around the corner were new joints and new scenes that hadn't existed before. They sprung up like weeds through asphalt. Though music groups descendant of the Beatles still ruled the airwaves, we songwriters in the supposedly unsophisticated sidetrack called "Texas" had the gigs.

And like islands on the plains some of the best friends we musician/writers had were TV producers who would put us on air whether we had tunes on the new FM stations or not. It might have been after the Farm Report on Sunday morning at 6:00 a.m., but we could tell interested parties we were on the tube nonetheless.

Bruce Bryant and Tony Bruni had one of the first songwriter-friendly music programs in the state with *The Little Ol' Show.* So even if I couldn't land a gig playing this month, I had a reputable place to show my wares that could help me get work . . . next month.

I returned to Houston with a distinct appreciation for those dusty little saloons, new or old, that dotted the badder sides of town. At least they paid in cash what little you could make playing to eight people on an early weeknight. The heir to a couple of generations of them, and what is now the longest-lived in one location, was Anderson Fair Retail Restaurant. Right place, for a long time. It was like an Internet you drove a Volkswagen to for a wealth of us Texas writers in the steamy, stormy '70s.

Imagine those ambitious mornings of the Montrose musician for a moment. You can almost smell the Cuban coffee at Cardet's as much as the alcohol on your breath. Hand me the ashtray: Dusty and Rocky Hill, Lightnin' Hopkins, Mance Lipscomb, Juke Boy Bonner, Townes Van Zandt, Guy Clark, Don Sanders, John Carrick, David Rodriguez, Wrecks Bell, Mickey White, Peter Gorisch, Darryl Harris, Rich Layton, Kent Cole, Teri Greene, Jim Raycraft, Rock Romano, Ezra Idlet, John Grimaudo, Keith Grimwood, Gary Parker, Walt and Harry, Dale Barton, Reb Smith, Bob Sturtevant, Danny Everitt, Robbie Fields, Susan Clark, Michael Marcoulier, Frank Davis, Stephen Jarrard, Franci Files, Andre Mathews, Bill and Lucille Cade, Denise Franke, Bill Staines, Shake Russell, Dana Cooper, John Vandiver, Michael Mashkes, Blaze Foley, Robert Earl Keen, Ron Crick, Bill Haymes, Jack Saunders, Rick Gordon, Doug Lacey, Joe Lindley, Pam Grimes, Dan Earhart, Lynn Langham, Sean Walters, Lucinda Williams, Connie Mims, Nanci Griffith, Roger Ruffcorn, Eric Taylor, Richard Dobson, Lyle Lovett, Don Becker, Steve Beasley . . . and me.

♪ *VII* ♪

Secret Mountain Laboratory

*I*n the mid-'70s my girlfriend was a DJ named "Slowly Grail." At the time I never knew just what that meant. In time I learned it didn't matter. She did shows for a Pacifica station, KPFT, downtown on Prairie Street. We lived with Harriet Heaton, an early owner of Anderson Fair, and DJ Richard Brooks, a.k.a. Ace Paladino, different shift, same station, as well as being the lightman at Liberty Hall.

So it was a somewhat communal and rockin' two-story house with a huge sound system that would easily, and often did, play the neighborhood. Daily we disappeared into the Montrose on our own separate, consuming missions. Around dinnertime, a six pack of beer and a joint were like a bug light. Guaranteed to attract. Nightly we saw one another at the clubs.

Back then these pals, "Slow" and "Ace," let us play live on KPFT at almost a moment's notice. While we endured our respective art scenes to the next party tray, I performed for tips and free lunches at Anderson Fair. That always included plenty of day-old garlic bread and the other major food groups: spaghetti and beer.

Then when you think it can't get any better, a Deadhead from Phoenix with money to burn started up a radio station in Lake Tahoe, California, just across the state line from Nevada, in Kings Beach. It was 12 miles from Truckee and practically on the north shore of Lake Tahoe itself. DJs from all over the U.S. and one from Radio Caroline off-shore of England came there to spin records and yuk it up in the Sierra.

We were off to play radio at the Secret Mountain Laboratory, KSML, in a green 1960 VW camper with our two dogs: Osso, the black lab and Buffy, the Australian Heeler. With a five-gallon propane tank on the roof of the camper that ran by hose to a double burner on a counter behind the rider seat, I made Cuban coffee in an espresso pot while "Slow" drove. When we were trucking down the highway and it got really cold, I lit both burners. That car had no heater . . . and no fire extinguisher either.

The radio station was on Lake Tahoe Boulevard, with the control-room window looking out onto the lake. We moved three blocks away to a little wood cabin on Snake Street. It stood among the tall, orderly spruces in the shadow of the mountain peaks that surrounded the 30-mile long lake. I wrote and recorded new songs almost daily at the cabin on a cheap cassette machine. The gigs were few and far be-tween. I spent more time in the casinos gambling with the 75 cents off the top of a weekly paycheck than I did gigging. Probably won more money on keno than I did playing music. At least at the casino the drinks were free if you were nice to the wait staff.

Now and again we would go down to San Francisco. I played a few of my tunes with David Grisman at his house in Marin, and was part of a huge entourage backstage with the Grateful Dead at one of their last Winterland gigs. A marvel of controlled confusion, backstage was like a schoolyard the width and height of a basketball court with chil-dren bouncing about while Mom and Dad, and various other mem-bers of the band, stood in private huddles here and there smoking spliffs the size of their thumbs. Periodically they would exhale, laugh, and point at their children's antics. This date further turned me on to live electric guitar. Jerry Garcia made it look off-the-cuff in front of thousands of fans, and I admired what those Californians could do with guitars that looked like surfboards.

Back up in the Sierra, I played every chance I could get. Unfortunately for my wallet, I teed it up mostly in Tahoe City for tips at a vegan place called Nectar Madness. I played in a Truckee restaurant for cheap hippie jewelry. I even tuned it up in a dusty Silver City, Nevada, bar in the middle of the desert whenever the opportunity arose—mostly when the Harleys arrived from the Bay Area. For a couple of years, me and that soulful silhouette of a dark top kept the home fires burning.

But that's where my lover and I split the sheets. She kept the shift at the radio station. I took Buffy and the guitar back to that criminal territory, Texas, to start a band of my own. I was a little hot about the bad luck of my latest love and I was moving back to one of the hottest, most humid places there was. You could fry an egg on the sidewalks of Texas. In Houston they'd poach.

♪ *VIII* ♪

Six Strings, No Kick

I'd been playing that acoustic guitar long enough for it to look like a Brazilian-rosewood-and-spruce extension of my rib cage. It was where all the songs I wrote came from. Nevertheless, I wanted to add new tunes to my repertoire. I wanted to play with other like-minded musicians. I wanted to interpret the music I had loved since I was a kid, as well as write music I hoped was just as good. Musicians made far more money in Texas playing the hits in pickup bands out in the interstate motel lounges. That wasn't quite what I had in mind. Instead, I wanted to be more like the glamorous rock 'n' rollers in the British Invasion that had shrewdly marketed Houston kids like me since I was old enough to tune an AM radio.

I happened upon a rough-looking, blonde Rickenbacher guitar hanging on a pawnshop wall in Houston. It was similar to the one Lennon played in the early Beatles. It was puppy love, alright. It had some important pieces missing but still had the original pickups. A few trips to the guitar fixer later and it was reconditioned plenty good enough for four-by-four rock 'n' roll, even without the whammy bar. For the first time in my young performing career, I played both the familiar, woody 28 and the new, loud, and raucous member of the orchestra.

In 1976, after moving back to Houston from Tahoe, I scoured the Montrose neighborhoods for eligible types with my own developing tastes to form a band. The result was my first group, a five-piece called The Level Flight Band. We had a drummer, Jim Alderman, a bassist, Peter Gorisch, a lead guitarist, Steve Beasley, and Dan Earhart a.k.a. "Captain Macho" on keys and a Celeste which we called the "portable door bell." It was like a glockenspiel with a keyboard. I probably destroyed at least a couple of other groups in putting this wild bunch together.

In short and rather breathless order we learned a repertoire of Vince Bell fingerpicking and flat-pick strummers. I added a smattering of Warren Zevon, Nick Lowe and Dave Edmonds, Little Feat, Bob Dylan, the Rolling Stones, and the ever-so Beatles. I played the heavier sounding numbers like Zevon's "Lawyers, Guns, and Money" through a Twin Reverb amp look-alike with that pawn shop wall-hanging. After a while, the dreadnaught sat in its stand most of the night.

My band members and I were ambitious to the point of bodily harm. When you're that young, you may well fail miserably but you ain't gonna die. We threw ourselves at showbiz like stage divers. We began to be the recognizable carnival characters in the dilapidated localities off the beaten paths of Houston and I was as clown-faced as any of them.

But it was my name on the marquee, so it was up to me to find the watering holes that would book us sight unseen, using a phone Southwestern Bell disconnected with almost clockwork regularity. We unstoppable boys were long on *want to* but short on just *how to* go about it. And whatever we did while inventing our take on show business, we did with nothing at all. That was good art. Something from nothing.

After scheduling a few openers with Mike Condray at his 500-seat Liberty Hall in Houston, which netted the band some fair reviews from the local papers, we were on our way to that collegiate capital town in the Hill Country. I took my game but inexperienced bunch to play in Austin, scoring a gig at Castle Creek in Armadillo World Headquarters town. We were going to open for singer Doug Sahm and his equally well-known piano player, Augie Meyers. Now that was moving on down the highway. I was going to play with a charting rocker, one of Texas' favorites. Pretty exotic fare. My first half-dozen years playing had mostly been as a solo. Now I was fronting a band.

When the day of the gig arrived, we stuffed the old camper with as much equipment and warm bodies as we could. The rest of us piled into my Rambler. About four in the afternoon, we pulled up to the club and I threw open the doors of the van on Guadalupe. The asphalt was almost molten in the relentless Texas sun. My tennis shoes stuck to it and I could've been fingerprinted in it.

The jumble of amps and music paraphernalia that appeared when the doors yawned open looked like a garage sale on wheels. The band and I resembled a line of ants as we methodically lowered our heads and hauled the heavy boxes, cymbals, stands, and drum cases until we were sweating. The smell of stale beer and body odor that came from the closed-up honky-tonk made us all feel right at home for the first time in 150 miles. It was just like some of the flophouses we played back down on the Gulf Coast.

As some of the fellows stacked our tattered speaker enclosures stage-side, I slipped into the back room to check out the accommodations for the bands. There was a couch that had seen a far better day and some folding metal chairs around a swimming-pool-shaped, particleboard coffee table that looked like it had come out of a *Dick Van Dyke Show.* The walls were hung with morosely colored drapes. The lone table lamp had obviously been on the floor, and often. It hung like a scarecrow with its arms flailing, but shone like a 40-watt beacon. The rug stuck like gum to the soles of your shoes from the beer and mixed drinks that had been spilled on it. The accompanying bathroom on the alley-side wall of the joint smelled to high heaven and was out of the question. I couldn't stay. When I came out, I feigned a positive face. My shoes sounded like the bottoms were covered with Velcro on the carpeted floor of the club. Rip, rip, rip.

I cavalierly sauntered up to the bar. My bandmates were changing strings and arranging the stage. They watched me with dry mouths. I motioned with as much savvy as I could muster at the barkeep for a cold one. With a swipe of an obscenely stained rag across a big wooden banister, he scowled, "The bar ain't open, sonny." So much for having any clout at all when you're the opening act.

After we completed the sound check, the guys and I wilted on that smelly couch and tossed our set list and a change of clothes on the coffee table. Our shoes made sucking noises as we paced back and forth.

For better or worse, for a few anonymous moments, we owned the joint. We threw our string sets, flat picks, shoulder straps, guitar cords, drum pads, drumsticks, foot pedals, and tuners on the table. Things were arranged just so for everyone. You set it up like you wanted it because it was the only thing you could do to be comfortable in such an unfriendly-feeling place.

Then the word wafted over us from one of the bartenders that the headlining band had arrived. They came in like a private conversation. Unlike my high-spirited, enthusiastic boys, they were specters. You could look square at them but you never quite got a glimpse at their faces. The famous singer and the piano player were nowhere to be seen.

"Hi, my name is . . ."

"Move!"

"No problem." Good manners just won't get it here. Welcome to the pros.

As if versed in jungle warfare, they silently stalked into the place virtually unseen. By the time they reached the stage, my wide-eyed boys were fidgeting around the door to the back room. They re-sembled overmatched and underweight boxers before a real beating. They were too nervous to sit while the headliners took over the place. When they shouted for a beer, they got one. When the drummer wanted a towel, it arrived in a heartbeat in the hand of one of the club owners. It was a food-chain thing. The top predators had arrived.

After they sound-checked sans the heralded singer and the keyboard player they moved in slow motion off stage left and disappeared into that back room. A couple of my boys were back there, so, protective, I made a beeline backstage. Sahm's band circled the coffee table like coyotes eyeing my band's collection of music paraphernalia. They picked up a flat-pick or a capo here and there like they were grazing. They eyed the tuner, a chorus ensemble, and the keys to the Rambler as they modeled my bass player's Hawaiian shirt among themselves. These San Antonio fellows dressed in Harley Davidson T-shirts and leathers were missing only bandoleros and revolvers. Their long black braids glistened in the beer lights. They laughed from way down in their bellies. And finally they took a string or two to go along with the capo, pads of paper, and pens. No questions. They scribbled a "to go" order on the back of one of our set lists. We were quiet as hell as they passed it and a couple of bills to some gofer who lit out like a gazelle for the closest McDonald's. The glaring musicians grunted like bull sea lions as they collapsed on that nasty couch in front of their many beers.

I felt the compressor for the air conditioner kick over. The whole place shuddered like someone had dropped a great weight on to the cement floor. A huge blower in the wall belched some acrid atmo-sphere from a thousand nights before. But it was more than welcome as it slowly began to refrigerate that stifling tinderbox of a joint. The temperature dropped like a stone. When the hairs in your nose froze, you couldn't smell the room anymore. After that I carried an oscillat-ing fan as standard equipment.

My fellows stood around with their fists clenched in silent, thirsty, and now hungry but indignant postures. The poor possessions that once sat on the table now stuck out of the tops of the leather vest pockets for all the world to see. They finally acknowledged our existence with a menacing cut of the eye. As if on cue, we instantly exhaled a forced laugh and found something terribly interesting to watch near the ceiling. These were probably the first people I had ever seen in leather pants in the summer in Texas, outside of a magazine.

All's well that just ends. And the gig went just fine. After we played, they treated us like real people when we came offstage. Apparently we had passed muster. "No, really, that's OK. Just keep the chorus ensemble."

We hardly noticed when Doug and Augie finally arrived, moments before they were to take the stage. They never even saw the back room. For the entire second set, the pop singer was wailing away in front of that nine-piece band with a brass section of saxophone, trombone, and trumpets, while the piano player was hunkered over, passed out. He was exhausted from touring, laid out cold drunk and bent over on the Farfisa electric piano. The poor casualty landed where he fell. His band played on like this was part of the show.

We went back to Houston. I had a new maturity about my business behind a guitar. I was turning into a writer, a different person than the teen idols I had tried to emulate with my group. It would ultimately take a few more dips into the pond of my imagination, a place I never spent much time in the shallow end of. But I was becoming liberated from delusions of my youth. An acoustic guitar, because of the creative freedom it had always offered, was the thing I coveted above all else and held on to the hardest.

My trusty guitar had been relegated to playing backup to a pawn shop thrill. Ian McLagan asked the question in a tune called "La De La": "Do you believe in livin' other people's dreams?" Though the acoustic guitar didn't fit so well with the popular music of the '60s it was part of me like something skintight when I began to perform in the '70s, and every year after that. It was the companion I wrote with, be it a ballet or a barroom ballad. It was a complete compositional tool that reflected my work as well as being something to stand behind in the heat of a Saturday night.

So all through the '70s, through the Beatles, and the British Invasion, through Northern California and the bands I put together, it became clearer. If I was going to survive my budding authorship in the rough-and-tumble music world, if I was going to make the difference I aspired to with my work, it would be because I kept playing those solo gigs. Just me and those six strings. No kick.

♪   *IX*   ♪

Three-Day Ride to the Kitchen

*I*n late 1976 I decided on a move to Austin to work as a singer/songwriter for Moon Hill Management. It was just in time for the Progressive Country days, and I was booked all over Texas doing half-music, half-comedy shows wherever they would pay me. It seemed my songs could keep me in places I could barely negotiate on my own. With my unsophisticated voice like a high-school quarterback, every little bit helped. But after enough years of choir-boy vocals, Bob Dylan taught us in the '60s that the voice didn't have to matter as much as the message did.

Craig Hillis from Moon Hill picked me up outside the Greyhound bus station the day I moved to that capital town. With me was my bag holding everything I had in the world. Right beside my bag was the guitar in the case with the grommets missing, the alligator linen covering all but gone. Craig liked the songs he had heard on the confusion of tapes made in the cabin off Lake Tahoe and was impressed when he saw the hard-livin' acoustic come out of the frayed case. We became the closest of friends. After sleeping on a couple of couches, I rented a two-room grandmother house behind a funeral home on

North Lamar. I was across the road from another popular radio station, KOKE, and no more than a couple of blocks from Moon Hill.

The routine each day was to walk or bike to the booking agent. I'd stand around, cup of coffee in hand, with road managers of several other acts and other artists funneling into meetings with the business manager, Larry Watkins, or the publisher, Tom White. My goal was always to find work. Sometimes if you didn't squeak like a rusty gate, you didn't work like a musician.

I had seen plenty of my home state on my own, but I probably saw more of Texas during the early Austin years than I ever cared to know was there. Some of it was in Louisiana, Arkansas, and Colorado. With nothing but me and the six-string, like sacrificial lambs, we would warm up for bands at the 500- to 1,500-seat concerts, then traipse off and do our own nights at smaller clubs.

I was billed at the Armadillo World Headquarters and all of the joints in the Austin and Houston areas at one time or another, and in clubs named Steamboat Springs in multiple locations, to Liberty Lunch and Gruene Hall. I was booked more than once at the Austin Opera House, the Texas Opry House, Hoffeinz Pavilion, Auditorium Shores, the Special Events Center, Cullen Auditorium, Liberty Hall, and at 110-degree summer outdoor shows at racetracks all over the state from Fredericksburg to Nacogdoches. I performed more times than I can recall in Dallas and San Antonio. Was born in the one city and never had one good gig in the other until the next century.

It was always such a challenge to show up before the big, seven-piece band that was the main bill and duke it out with a front row filled with impatient entertainment shoppers. They never wanted anything to do with the opener because the opener was a no-name and probably wasn't any good anyway. Nor did they care to wager their cover charge to find out. Nothing between me and that brain trust but six strings on a wooden box. Now that's swingin' without a net. I'd usually wax like a romantic about things I had no business trying to wax about in the first place. Live and learn.

This is where the comedy part of a one-man, one-guitar show could save your dusty butt. Steven Fromholz and I spent a decade together pulling that off in the least amusing places, like a tacky Central Texas fern bar for trendy chicks in a shopping mall next to a department store near an army base. Did I forget anything?

"Frogboltz," as we all called him in lighter moments, was my closest friend in music during these late '70s Austin years. Steven was already a legend, and I was very proud when we were first booked together. As a writer of music and lyrics he was one of the finest. We became very compatible on- and offstage. We shared meals, we shared tequila, we shared friends, and sometimes we even drove to the dates together, laughing and burning along the way. I babysat his daughter Felicity when I needed a couple of extra bucks. Steven was urbane, very eloquent, graceful, and capable as a performer. Out on the mirage of the mesquite plains there was no one bigger-hearted.

"It was the 'Great Progressive Country Scare' of the mid-'70s," says Steven. "Where the hippie met the redneck over a cold beer with a joint. That was the fan base we played to. You took those long-haired hippie weirdos, and you had the rednecks, and they got together—they all liked Willie Nelson and they all liked to drink a cold beer—and you ended up with a bunch of great big, broad-shouldered, long-haired, kick-ass hippies.

"We were on the road all the time, playing music, drinking whiskey, and smoking pot. I had had a hit with my song 'I'd Have to Be Crazy' on Willie's album and it was rockin' and rollin'. When I wasn't out playing with the band, I did a lot of work with Vince, all over Texas, because I really loved his music. We were young—hell, I was barely 30, and Vince was 26, 27. We all wanted to play, and we played everything we knew and made up shit, too. As Willie said, 'If we hadn't been able to play music, we'd all be stealing cars, all be hoodlums in jail. We're all too lazy to work.'

"Moon Hill was managing everyone in town. They had me under contract, Michael Murphy, Asleep at the Wheel. They put Vince and me together on dates all over the circuit: Austin, Houston, the Pink Flamingo in Wichita Falls, The Irish Pub in Pueblo, Colorado, the old Poor David's in Dallas. Those were the halcyon days, and it didn't get any better than Poor David's. Wall-to-wall people. Wall-to-wall women, what a view—God almighty! You couldn't move in the room, people were sitting on the floor. Smokey. And we'd just kill them. Me and VB would just kill them. We used to tear that place down.

"We made some great music, too. One of the best songs I've ever heard is Vince's 'Sun & Moon & Stars.' We used to get together, usually drunker than hell in the motel room after the gig, and I'd make Vince sing that song. It's what friends are all about, and it's said so well in that song."

Those were years when the weekend days were Monday and Tuesday 'cause we were probably playing and then driving the old pickup back from somewhere between Shreveport and El Paso on Friday, Saturday, and Sunday. Those musicians' off-days were the laundry days, when Steven and I would sit against the same dirty window in the same rundown, un-air-conditioned Laundromat at 29th and Guadalupe in Austin. Fromholz could really fold those contour sheets.

Then there were the better times. Prior to my own gigs in Evergreen, Winter Park, and Steamboat Springs, Colorado, Delbert McClinton and I did a date at a joint called The Hungry Farmer in Boulder. I was the solo opener for him and his band. The next morning he invited me to his motel room to play a few of my songs. While I tuned to an A440 tuning fork, we talked like Texans far from home. He confided that he once showed "one a' them Beatles" some licks on the harmonica. I was fascinated to hear him. No doubt, that was Lennon.

I played him a song. At least a little surprised, he said, "Just a minute, I got to go put a shirt on."

What a great guy, I thought.

So I played him another.

♪ ✗ ♪

The Songwriter

*T*hroughout all the luck, good and bad, I wrote songs. I wrote them in the kitchen, in the car, in the evening, on holidays, but mostly when it was inconvenient. A lot of the work I put into a new tune was done when trying to sleep, before I would wake for the day and put my thoughts to the test. I have always had collections of ideas and tunes penned in an "idea cache" of Black Books. They were the enduring, final resting place for all kinds of recollections, reflections, and the thoughts that occurred day-to-day. By my observation, it took eight pages of cross-outs to be able to settle on three four-line verses and a refrain.

Writing is not writing at all. It's editing windy cliché and dogtrot verse. It's taking what you so loved the day before and, with a fastball-throwing motion, tossing the miserable piece of trash into the can in the corner. Sometimes songs take 60 minutes. Sometimes songs take six years. Further, when you finally get down to it, it's not what you write, it's what you don't write. It's as important to know what you don't want as it is to know what you do. Lastly, when you learn to write the pause, the spaces between the words become as influential as the words themselves. But I don't know how much can really be said about something that never happens the same way twice.

Songs have always thronged around me like famished birds. On the day I put the finishing touches to them, they fly away. As they leave, others take their place. There are always a half dozen of the perky little dears pestering me for attention. Then this morning I find yet another tiny, figurative fowl quietly preening itself on the edge of my desk.

THE SONGWRITER

You play like you practice.
It's not how long, it's how often.
One song teaches another.
So, it's not when you get it . . . it's that you get it.
Get it?

I still rarely did anything without my instrument. It was unfailingly around when I fishtailed a four-wheeler in the sand-filled storm drains of Midland, or when I saw the devastation after a tornado initialized one-mile swaths of Wichita Falls. It leaned up against a backroom table when I got my head stove in with bats by a marauding band of toughs in the parking lot of Anderson Fair.

I played that guitar in the same parking lot when I became the "Mayor of Montrose" after my set on the outdoor stage at an annual Montrose Area Block Party, the Woodstock in the tropics for a few thousand dye-dressed people. I was elected mayor by a cabal of the local elite, and the honor was receiving the Shoes of the Mayor, an awfully outsized pair of Oxfords that any two people I knew could fit in comfortably. These revered futons for the feet were painted by hippie chicks in hippie colors, with a lot of celestial pictographs and peace signs. Between block parties the shoes occupied a hallowed space atop an upright piano on the stage at Anderson Fair. The piano was probably painted by the same hippie chicks.

On yearly trips I drove the guitar, teeth clenched, into hurricanes to play dates in Corpus, Galveston, and Beaumont.

And I did most every kind of odd job imaginable. My dog, that guitar, and I sold fireworks out on a lonesome two-lane asphalt highway, living in the roll-away plywood enclosure for up to ten days and nights at a time during Christmas and New Year's. I wrote tunes in that long plywood box. I hung paper on people's doorknobs in the wards of the big southwestern towns so I could keep something edible in the house. I drove a cab, strung fence wire, bought guitars, squeegeed windows, dug postholes, sold guitars, cleaned boats, mowed lawns, did construction and landscaping, and everything else I could to keep my authorship alive.

It was a constant struggle from one gig to another, but I never did anything that felt below my station. My station was anywhere I had to be at a particular moment, so that I could continue. Rest on the laurels of last night's performance and you might not eat regularly even after the flattering review came out.

Only the musically inclined could find the cheapest gas known to man, the oldest car to put it in that would still make it to a gig, or the smallest apartment, trailer, or broken-down house to park beside, behind the tallest weeds on the block to hide your wheels from the car-thieving neighbors. If you couldn't pull this off, you rode the bicycle and hung it from the ceiling indoors. You knew *the* bargain at every restaurant, discount store, and grocery for miles around. In those days we could make a dollar stretch from between the Red and the Rio Grande to hell and back. Even so, from time to time it just wasn't far enough.

Elastic Plastic Fork and Pitiable Paper Plate

*I*n those days, one of the places you would always be welcome to play was the place that couldn't, or wouldn't, pay you any money. Money so that maybe you and that 28 could do it tomorrow. And there were the occasions where you teed it up for your buddies. The buddies remained the preeminent reason you started talking that talk with a dread on your hip in the first place. Sometimes you got a girlfriend, a place to stay, or something to eat. Bravo.

Cooking for sport, Texas style. In dear old Tejas they call it the Thanksgiving Rehearsal. It began in the 1970s and has been held every year, over three days, the weekend before the traditional Thursday in November, at a summer cabin on a lake in East Texas. After the rooms inside are spoken for, acres of people camp out on the large wooded property.

It's lasted as long as any music festival or flea market. It's attracted as many people from as many places as a political party. And it's as important to those who are lucky enough to be there as football is to Texas, no kidding. Over this feed you'd think you'd died and gone to heaven. You may die, but not of hunger. You only need an appetite and a musical instrument. But if your newest set of mediums are old as God's dog, the appetite will do. Anyway, no shortage of stringed things here.

While cowboy and cowgirl chefs jet in and out of the kitchen, everyone who isn't playing Texas music nonstop eats delicacies from Texas nonstop. Above freezing or below. Rain or snow.

On arrival, carloads un-crease from their ride and hang a conspicuous spoon around their neck. The menu for this musico-feast in the East Texas forest covers breakfast, lunch, and dinner, served in continuous waves on outsized picnic tables on the screened-in back porch.

That holiday butterball that Mother lovingly basted all those devoted hours and the trimmings pale by comparison. Quite honestly, they would be a snack at this gathering. The idea here for the cookers is to make not only large things but unforgettable small things as well. The idea for the "music types" is to be there when whatever it is comes out of the oven. Something you can actually get pretty good at. It's what it's all about when, after a night train of music, it's 7:30 in the morning, you can't see quite yet, and the breads have just come out of the oven. Navigation by sense of smell.

So here's where the spoon comes in. They issue each attendee a metal tablespoon, one time and one time only. Your name is engraved on the ringed handle that you tie a string through, and you hang the spoon from your neck. Between the bacons, and cheeses, and biscuits, and fudges, and cookies, and anything else you might imagine from most anyplace you've ever been, facts is facts. You can't handle the comestible onslaught with an elastic plastic fork and a pitiable paper plate.

Wherever you may wander over the weekend, you will be able to spoon a taste of something delightful from campsite to campsite on your way to the official meals served on the porch at the cabin. On Sunday they wheel a few trash cans full of iced oysters into the driveway and pass out shucks to the kids.

Drums stay permanently set up beside an old bookshelf-turned-light-stand and they're constantly in use. PA equipment towers to the ceiling in that music room just off the confusion of the kitchen. There's not a lot of room inside to breathe, much less loiter to, the raucous refrains of four-by-four rock 'n' roll plus those Texans cooking for thrills. Mostly, you end up outside listening to the band through an open window. The wall of the house becomes a huge sounding board.

And me? I amble from pup-tent to pop-up camper trying to find someone I don't know. Or won't by the time I leave. On the shore beside last night's bonfire, I find other familiars with fiddles, mandolins, string basses, banjos, harmonicas, and guitars. The woods around are alive with their melodies. I have my 28 over my shoulder, an illegal smile on my face, and someone's Lone Star beer in my hand.

♪ *XII* ♪

Bermuda Triangle

*F*un's funner 'n hell. My pals and I survived it for more than a decade. But as in all showbiz scenes, there's a fat lady. Willie Nelson was making hit recordings of some of my friends' tunes, but many had moved on to other places or became known for something other than country music as the '80s arrived. Anyway, we hadn't turned out country music. We'd turned out Texas music.

Those of us who stayed in Austin were becoming a rare breed. I didn't yet have any gray hair but I was working on it, and all the varnish was worn off the neck of the guitar. I was still playing the gigs and methodically writing the songs as the '80s slithered in. I was in another relationship and living in a small, shiplap frame house on a fifth of an acre with a hurricane fence. Things were intangibly getting harder, whether I could see them becoming different or not. The gigs became fewer and farther between, so I started pitching my songs for more varied forms of presentation.

I presented my idea for a ballet to James Clouser, the choreographer of Space Dance Theatre in Houston. It was named after one of my songs, "Bermuda Triangle," a dream-sequence song that formed the plot of the entire work. I had to catch up with him at a motel in the rain one day, but six months later he sold the idea to the City of Houston and the Moody Foundation. They financed the production and in May of 1980 it was presented at Miller Outdoor Theatre in Houston's Herman Park. I played the music live during the performances with Passenger, a jazz band, behind a 40-foot-tall scrim. Thirty thousand people saw the four-night run of this ballet. I had never played a show that big before.

BERMUDA TRIANGLE

While you were sleeping,
I was reading
this book about Bermuda.
My eyes grew sleepy
and tired of reading,
I drifted past the moon.

How 'bout you, how 'bout you? How 'bout me?

While you were sleeping,
the sky was weeping,
the stars fell to the ground.
Lightning bolted, the ocean opened,
and swallowed me right down.
The earth grew silent, a tiny bubble
of breath before my eyes.

Glistening roundly,
a chorus called me
closer to the light.
I spied around me a thousand armies
as still as death could lie.
Breasts of armor,
wheels of fire,
drowned by weight of time.

Up swelled a specter,
a mighty vision
that swept across the sky.
The chamber rippled, gables crumbled
as ancient ages cried.
Who are we, where are we, who am I to be here?

While you were sleeping,
I was reading
this book about Bermuda.

In a review of the ballet, the *Houston Chronicle*'s Charles Ward said, "*Bermuda Triangle* opens as a traveler dies and witnesses his own funeral, one much like a New Orleans jazz funeral in which the people are sad that he's gone and happy he's gone to heaven. The man then goes on a journey in which he faces various aspects . . . of the unconscious mind. The traveler finds that the archetypal characters change faces (i.e., the angel becomes an executioner). Only when all these transformations are faced is the traveler ready to return to reality."

James Clouser wrote in the program notes: "Imagine being brought face-to-face with your worst fears and then finding that the demons that are attacking you from the outside are your own creations, and you can only get rid of them by embracing them." The macabre irony of the story's similarity to what was about to become my own would be lost on me for a good while to come.

♪   *XIII*   ♪

Name Unknown

Admit Date: 12-21-82

Admit Time: 02:12 a.m.

Multiple trauma patient transported from scene of MVA—found lying, face-down on ground—unconscious but breathing spontaneously. Male in 20–30 age range. Name unknown.

2:30 Dr. C. notified at home

2:50 Dr. W. notified

Preoperative Diagnosis: Multiple System Injury with Hemoperitoneum. Postoperative Diagnosis: Multiple Liver Lacerations.

Operation Performed: Exploratory alparatomy, repair multiple liver lacerations and bilateral tube thoracostomies. Because of the patient's closed head injury, no further surgery was done at this time, particularly the forearm fracture and the scalp laceration were left intact and the patient was moved to the CAT Scan room as quickly as we possibly could.

Patient was taken to the operating room where general anesthesia was induced, abdomen prepped and draped in the usual fashion, including the chest. Midline incision was made carried down to the free peritoneal cavity which was full of clotted and unclotted blood. Numerous liver lacerations were present and repaired with O chromic catgut in the usual fashion. Lacerations were confined to the right lobe, particularly the dome, and along the falsiform ligament. The remainder of the abdomen including the stomach, pancreas, duodenum, small bowel, colon, retroperitoneal area were all normal. Spleen was normal. Diaphragms were normal. Jackson Preatt drain and a Penrose drain were utilized, brought out through stab incisions of the right flank. Wound closed with running L Proline, skin with staples; bilateral tube thorocostomies were performed, causing multiple rib fractures bilaterally because patient will be on ventilator.

6:15 Multiple trauma MVA admitted to ICU #9 from CT Scan. DX SMI, Fx arm, Scalp lacerations, and post-op repair liver laceration. Left pupil larger than right. Both round and reactive to light and sluggishly beginning to move and shiver slightly. Does not open eyes to verbal or painful stimuli. Sterile touch wrap to head saturated and bloody drainage. Skin warm to cool and pale in color. Temp 97. Right arm casted, fingers bleeding slightly. Moving right fingers spontaneously.

7:00 Ice pack right arm.

7:45 Eyes open to speech. Right pupil smaller than left, sluggish to react; lower half of sclera and iris opaque.

8:00 To CT Scan

8:30 Drs. C. and B. here, discussing scalp laceration

9:30 Bath and linen changed

9:45 Redress head wound

10:00 IV site care; fan on right arm

11:00 Dr. B. talked to; Dr. H. here

11:30 Scalp and right eyebrow laceration sutured

12:00 Dr. R. here

2:00 Dr. G. here—right ulnar A-line inserted

4:00 Does not open eyes, pupils smaller, becoming very purposeful

6:00 Remaining semi-comatose, being purposeful

8:00 Semi-comatose. Will not open eyes even to painful stimuli. Does not follow commands. Pupils both round and react sluggishly. Opaque film noted over right eye. Moves all extremities spontaneously.

12:00 Opened eyes, left larger than right, to verbal stimuli. Moving everything with lag of left leg. Hard grip and release but not consistently.

2:00 a.m. Head dressing removed. Malodorous yellow-green contents noted on dressing. Cleaned sutures and head.

3:00 Head dressing removed and shampoo done; sutures re-cleaned and redressed.

6:30 Dr. B. here. Moving all extremities well except left leg drag; purposeful movements. Pupils now equal and round but difficult to assess reaction of eye due to opaqueness and film.

Hershel Cunningham ran a recording studio in Austin, Texas, in the '70s and early '80s. He was from up around Wichita Falls on the Oklahoma border. His studio was one of the premier places in the Lone Star State to put your best musical foot forward. It was called Riverside Sound.

My reputation as a musical maverick behind the acoustic guitar was solid. Richard Mullen, Tom Taylor, and Andy Salmon from the successful Austin group Christopher Cross were sold on some of my work. They and Kathleen Vick, my manager then, brought me into the studio to record three songs. The first notes to be recorded were from my guitar. Then the more famous fellows had taken over and embellished on my themes until we almost had a finished recording project, with arrangements of background vocals and whole groups of players contributing. At the time, I thought it might just be enough to put my work in the limelight for a showbiz moment. Surviving the southwestern music scene in downtown bars, uptown concert clubs, and country-and-western palaces out on farm roads had recommended me for the privilege.

The songs we chose related thematically to the pop music of the day and were ones that would benefit the most from a full-band arrangement. These three tunes took their own spaces, different from one another. They were from different eras of my authorship and displayed different capabilities.

Three guitarists, one per tune, played the breaks for the songs. Eric Johnson showed us all the elevating signature lick, patterned after the Livingston Baldwin arrangement of the song. Stevie Ray Vaughan just plain old tuned up and leveled the area around the studio with his soaring Strat. I swear some of the notes he hit just aren't included on a guitar of that model. Chris Holzhaus grooved, and grooved, and grooved.

The several sessions wound down to the reference vocals that were on the agenda for the night. After the evening's recording, I relaxed and confidently loaded the car with my Martin. I now kept it in a baggage-handler-proof, teardrop-shaped fiberglass case that the guitarist, one-time manager, and old friend Craig Hillis had loaned me. It was Christmas week, the early morning of December 21, 1982. I drove away from those comfortable, crowded sessions with respectful and talented friends into a haze of forgotten, trackless years where no one I knew had ever been. Little prepared me for the odyssey that calm holiday night had in store.

Less than five miles from the recording studio, I was thrown 50 feet from the car I drove and left facedown in a pool of gasoline on a feeder road to Interstate 35 on the south bank of the Colorado River. Sirens moaned and lights flashed. Metal twisted to metal in groaning, plaintive attitudes. Pavement stretched and grated like sandpaper. There were taunting, scraping noises. There were casualties littered about with death and sorrow hanging in the air. Worst of all, there were survivors.

At the midnight stoplight of Riverside Drive, my wife Melody and I were mauled at more than 65 mph in the driver's-side door by a drinking driver whose nationality was never determined. My right arm was not recognizable and my liver had been forced out of my mid-section onto the pavement. There was substantial injury to my spinal cord and brain. I would have scar tissue in my eyeballs as a result of lying in the gasoline. My lungs were collapsed. My skin was punctured in various places. Bones in my right arm were destroyed up to the elbow. I would have to be sculpted over again by armies of doctors and years of therapies to come.

And then I died.

In those hours of no man's land between night and day, some poor kid doing obits for the local paper, the *Austin American-Statesman*, happened by to find that I had made the list of the deceased earlier. He went back to the graveyard shift to turn in his predawn report for the morning news. My death made the daybreak edition.

As they say in showbiz, "As long as they spell the name right."

Twenty minutes later I resumed the rhythm if not the rhyme, aided by the wizardry of modern medicine.

My then-manager Kathleen Vick recalls, "Somebody called my brother Hank early that morning and said, 'Did you hear what happened? Vince Bell's been killed in a car wreck.' Hank had a friend visiting whose father was a police captain. He phoned his father, who said yes, he'd heard about it, and certainly those people hadn't lived.

"I remember thinking to myself, I have to pull myself together. I have to go identify the body and make some arrangements. I have to do something. At the time, I just took the news that Vince was dead as the gospel. And I was just on stun. Just automatic stun.

"I showed up at the hospital. I remember walking up the long ramp where the old emergency room used to be at Brackenridge. There were two policemen there talking. I stopped and asked them, 'Where do I go? A friend of mine was in an accident this morning.'

"One of the officers said, 'You know, they made it through that. They're still alive. That boy is still alive.' I beat my way up there and started going through the rigmarole from this desk to that. I find out yes, indeed, Vince is still alive. They're all giving it the shake-the-head routine, but yes, he's here. He's still alive.

"Then I just remember waiting a lot and the staff telling me that he was still alive but totally unconscious. They didn't know the extent of it, and they were not very hopeful at all. They were basically telling me the bottom line was that the injuries were so extensive that even if he did make it, there were probably going to be some real problems. They were trying to say that as nicely as they could, but I started getting the picture that Vince had a serious brain injury, and that they were almost saying that it might be better if he didn't live.

"Of course, I didn't want to hear that. If he was alive, Vince was going to be all right. That's the way it was. I just remember sitting by myself in a big room with metal chairs and tile floors. Just sitting there. It seemed like forever.

"Finally they told me they had him in intensive care and said, 'You can see him for two minutes, Ms. Vick.' There was nobody else there yet, so in I went. It was terrible. I couldn't really see him because he was covered in machines and bandages. I couldn't tell what was going on. He was all bandaged up and looked so pitiful in that bed, like a mummy, and he was just pitiful, all these things done to him. It broke my heart."

My sister Shary was living in Houston. "I got a call about 10 the next morning from Gary Don, Vince's wife's brother. He told me Vince and Melody had been in an accident and that it was really bad. Vince had been thrown from the vehicle, but part of the engine had come through the front and trapped Melody's feet. The car spun around a few times—this is the way the cop later explained it to me—and her feet were damaged. Vince's body skidded all over the pavement with glass everywhere—there was glass imbedded—and her teeth were shaved off. They both had gasoline in their eyes. They had found her ID but until Gary Don initially identified Vince, he was just listed as Mr. A.

"Mom and Dad were in Michigan, and I didn't know how to reach them. An information operator happened to know the area and gave me a list of hotels. After several tries a desk clerk said, 'Well, as a matter of fact he's right here. They're checking out right now.'

"I told them that Vince had been in a bad accident and that they should not go home but straight to Brackenridge Hospital in Austin."

My own memories of that night were taken completely—I don't have them even today. I wouldn't remember anything of those weeks of recording sessions either. The vocal performances of that evening, made moments before my collision, would sit uncelebrated in my tape catalog at home for years to come. I would learn early on after my head injury that being able to forget is a fortunate defense mechanism the brain throws together in the worst of times to keep you from recollections more painful than perhaps you would care to wrestle with. Ironically, buried alongside the bad lay the good.

People have often asked if I had any out-of-body experience or any religious revelation. Nope. No trumpets, no flowing robes. Nothing good, bad, or otherwise. It was just quiet. Calm. Peaceful. Serene. Confident and purposeful in an otherworldly kind of way.

I'm alive today because of the crackerjack response of the Emergency Medical Service team that picked up my wrecked physical debris. They shuttled it to the emergency room of the county hospital that kept me through the tenuous hours and days that would follow.

Janice Rials Rogers was an anesthesia tech at Brackenridge when she wasn't playing music. "I was just getting to work, and a team of three or four staff members was running down the hall with a patient in a bed. The team was moving extremely fast, and I knew whatever was happening was really bad. I pressed my back up against the wall so they could get by. As they ran past me, I looked at the patient, wondering what was wrong. His head was completely bandaged, so all I could see was a swollen face. I blurted out, 'Vince Bell.' The team came to a screeching halt, and someone asked if I knew who this was. I said I didn't know him personally, but I had seen him play music years earlier in Houston at a public radio fundraiser. They asked if I was sure, and I said Vince had a unique look and I was positive it was him. I told them he was from Houston (or least I thought so), and he was a musician. They told me that he had been in a terrible car wreck and up till now they had had no idea who he was. They said they were going back to surgery to remove his right arm that had been severely damaged in the wreck. I just remember saying over and over, 'You can't cut his arm off, he's a musician. How will he survive all of this if he can't play his guitar?' I was really upset that what he loved doing the most would be over. To me, that would have been worse than the wreck. I kept telling them that they had to save his arm.

"They ran on down the hall and into surgery, and I went to the OR to see if my group needed any help. The decision had been made to try to save his arm. They had no idea if the surgery would work, but at least they were willing to give it their best try.

"I checked on Vince in the recovery room many times throughout that day and went to his room on several occasions just to check on him. My husband and I moved to New Mexico not long after that and I didn't hear any news about him for years."

That flattering recognition saved my right arm. It was so demolished that the attending physicians were electing to cut the unrecognizable mess off. When they realized it had been essential to my lifework, they left it for another doctor to attempt to rebuild later. If I was ever going to have a chance of writing my name or feeling the neck of that fine guitar—much less playing music again—the miracle began there with Janice.

As I lay comatose in a tub of ice water to lower my brain-impairing fevers during those fragile days, my arm was over the edge of the tub dripping blood into a bucket.

ORTHOPEDIC HISTORY AND PHYSICAL EXAM

The patient has multiple injuries which have been taken care of, but his orthopedic injuries include multiple abrasions and bruises, but mainly both bones of the right forearm with a good radial pulse. Closed head injury with no evidence of definite injury or neurological loss, although could not really be evaluated because the patient was asleep when first examined. Placed him in a large posterior splint, after hanging him in sugar tongs. Feel that patient will need to have an open reduction and internal fixation when medically feasible. At the point that I saw the patient he was having a laparotomy for internal bleeding and was to be sent directly to the CAT scanner for a head scan to determine if a neurosurgical procedure should be done. It was felt that prolonging the procedure any longer by doing an open reduction and internal fixation of his forearm at that point may jeopardize the patient's neurological status, therefore, if the patient does not need a neurosurgical procedure, will allow him to stabilize and do the forearm in a few days. All extremities were palpated and no gross motion or crepitation was noted.

"I heard initially that both Vince and Melody were DOA," says my dear friend Bob Sturtevant. "Then that Vince was, and then that they had brought him back. It was devastating not only to know that they were in an accident but that they were next to death."

"I just threw a couple of things in a bag, got in the truck and hauled ass," my sister Shary says. "It had taken me about an hour to find Mom and Dad and make all the phone calls trying to figure out what to do and to call Lisa [another of my sisters]. We made it to the hospital in the early afternoon."

Lisa remembers, "The hospital needed someone to make a positive ID of Vince. They took us into the critical care unit and asked us if there were any identifying marks on his body. His face was so swollen it was unrecognizable. I told them that he was missing the little toe on his left foot from a bicycle accident when he was a kid. They identified him by his missing toe."

Shary says, "When I was finally allowed to see Vince, I was just— Gary Don tried to prepare me—but he was just so gray. I mean, just gray. I was really scared and very worried.

"The doctors said that I might have to give consent in case they wanted to drill a hole in his head to relieve the pressure on his brain. I was so worried about that. It really bothered me. I started asking questions, 'Isn't there something else you could do? Is he going to come out of this? How's he going to be?'

"They said, 'We don't know, this is a closed-head injury,' and began to explain that there was so much they didn't know about closed-head injuries, and that they never knew how people were going to come out of them. They didn't even know if he was going to wake up. They said again that he had a lot of pressure on his brain, that his brain was really swollen inside his skull, and that they were considering drilling a hole through his skull to relieve the pressure.

"They also told me that they were giving Vince diuretics to try to relieve some of the fluid, some of the pressure, on the brain. They explained his other injuries to me and the things that they had done. They told me about his arm being crushed and that they didn't know what they were going to do about that. That was before I knew that they had thought about removing it.

"The day went on. Friends of Vince's were starting to show up, and it made me angry. I was so worried and didn't really know what to tell people. I didn't want to have to explain it over and over. I just wanted to tell them, 'Get out of here, leave us alone.'

"When my parents arrived, they found me in the waiting room. I warned them that Vince was really gray, that he was not moving, and he had a lot of tubes. I went on to explain what all the injuries were and my parents looked scared. They saw Vince then, and when they came out they were in shock, and they were crying. And then the doctors spoke to them as well. That's the first time I can ever really remember seeing worry on my father's face."

Kathleen says, "Another thing that worried me was that they'd done a tracheotomy and now had the tube in. I told the doctors, 'This man is a songwriter, he's a singer, a performer.' Of course what they were thinking was, Hey, if the guy makes it then we'll think about all that, right?

"As the days went on, they began to contemplate taking the tube out—he was still on life support—because it was going to cause damage. Bruising damage. I just kept thinking there's got to be another way. They ended up leaving it in for a long time. But they had to do it to save his life."

♪ *XIV* ♪

Rumor of My Demise

*T*he rumor of my demise certainly spread far. Larry Monroe, who has been a mainstay of the University of Texas' radio station for over 25 years, remembers, "I had been working at KUT for a little over a year and a half on December 20, 1982. That was my last night of work for a few days because I was flying back to my hometown for the Christmas holidays. I finished my blues program, 'Blue Monday,' at midnight and, early in the morning of the 21st, left the station. I pulled my old blue Chevy onto I-35 southbound and as I pulled off the freeway at the Riverside exit I could see several emergency vehicles with their lights flashing. A police car was blocking the lanes and an officer was diverting traffic. As I made my turn I could see the aftermath of a very nasty automobile accident. I only had a moment to look, but I could tell from the debris that it had been a pretty bad crash. I went on home and packed for my trip to Indiana.

"I got to the airport a few hours later and bought an *Austin American-Statesman* and slipped it into my carry-on bag. After I boarded the plane, I pulled out the paper as I sat waiting for takeoff. I remembered the accident that I had seen and I looked to see if it had made the early edition. And there it was in the headline: 'Austin Musician Vince Bell Killed In Auto Accident.' I read the piece just as the jet rolled down the runway and lifted off the tarmac into the sky. The article was about the accident that I had seen, and said Vince Bell had died at the scene from severe injuries. I looked to my right, out the window, at Austin receding as the plane climbed and thought about what I had just read. Vince was a prominent singer-songwriter in Austin and I had seen the aftermath of the car crash that had killed him.

"After I returned to Austin a week or so later I told a friend that I had seen the accident that Vince Bell had died in, and he interrupted me, 'Vince didn't die. He's in bad shape, but he is alive.' I said I had read in the paper the next morning that he had died at the scene, but my friend confirmed that Vince had, indeed, survived the accident and the report in the paper was incorrect. The paper I had bought at the airport was the earliest edition of the day, and all editions after that one omitted the mention. I was one of the few who had seen the incorrect report, and since I had read it on the way out of town I didn't learn the truth for several days."

Shary remembers, "From what I understood, Vince was dead at the scene and then revived. His liver was cut almost in half and he had a bad, bad closed-head injury. That car was mangled. EMS was on the scene a minute and a half later and was able to revive him. He was in surgery all night long."

In Houston, Tim Leatherwood, the owner of Anderson Fair and an old friend, was notified. "Eric Taylor called me and said in a hysterical voice that Vince had been killed in a car wreck. Of course, your first comment is, 'You're kidding?' Stupid comment, but nonetheless it usually comes out.

"Eric said, 'No, I just talked to somebody in Austin, and they've taken him to Brackenridge and he's dead.'

"I don't remember who I was with that night but we immediately broke out a bottle of Jack Daniels and began to drink—drink a fond farewell to the wild and wacky Vince Bell. And then, I believe it was within a couple of hours because we hadn't finished the damn bottle, I got another phone call. Hold everything, stop the presses."

My long-time and close friend Bill Browder concludes with his story, "The rumors were flying around Austin that Vince was dead. I figured that Don Sanders would know. I called Don in Houston and he said Vince wasn't dead but had been in a bad wreck. He told me where he was, and I went to the hospital. They hadn't really even cleaned him up yet. He was hooked up to all the tubes and respirator and everything, but there was still blood caked on his hair and on his skin. Obviously, they had done all the stuff to keep him going but it was gruesome. He looked like someone who had come in from battle and gone into one of those MASH units, and they'd very unglamorously done what they had to do just to keep him from dying."

"During that first week, Vince was in a coma, and they had him in an oxygen tent," Shary says. "Kathleen Vick brought in a tape of the sessions they had been recording because the doctors wanted everybody to try and get Vince to wake up, to stimulate him. There were so many people there, like a massive media blitz. My sister Lisa, my brother Gary—I remember his reaction when he first saw Vince—I don't think he recognized him. Gary was shaken, and you didn't see Gary shaken very often. That really affected me. Gary was usually so tough.

"David Rodriguez was there, and a radio DJ I don't remember. Joe Preistnitz came in with Kathleen. Tim Leatherwood showed up at one point. And there were a lot of people that I didn't know. Everybody had to get in and see Vince. It's not like he didn't have family: 'We don't care about y'all, WE want to get in to see Vince. Let us get in, we're his family.' I mean, I wasn't rude, but I do remember thinking to myself on many occasions, Who do these SOBs think they are? What right do they think they have?

"We were all saying all kinds of things, pinching his toes, grabbing his hand, and he would respond. His eyes would move or maybe sometimes a tear would come out. It was hard to tell whether it was the fluid that they put in his eyes to keep them from getting dried out or whether it might be a tear. You couldn't say. He would wince.

"We could only see him for ten minutes every four hours. And there weren't supposed to be more than two people, but most of the time we had three. We were breaking the rules left and right, and making friends with lots of people in the ICU waiting room. A lot of other families were in there. Some of them weren't as lucky as we were. It's weird how people come together when you don't even know each other, when you have something like that in common.

"Anyway, Kathleen brought in the tape of the recording session Vince had been making every day, and Bill Browder brought in a ghetto blaster to play it on. Bill was there a lot. He was great. He was effective with Vince. Vince really responded to Bill."

"The expression on Vince's face is what I will always remember," says Bill Browder. "It was like he was pissed off that this had happened, and there was what I would characterize as a look of grim determination. I knew he always had that kind of chutzpah, and he had this look on his face like, By God, this isn't going to get me. I mean, right from the get-go. At first his face was just a bloody mess, but then it kind of stretched out and became more relaxed. But it was clear that here was somebody that had really been hammered and was in a coma. And you know how these comas are—some people just don't wake up.

"That was my concern, that if the initial injuries didn't turn him into a vegetable, it was going to be a matter of coming out of the coma. I felt he needed encouragement, so I took my ghetto blaster down there and played some songs that we'd written together. I poked at him and talked to him. It wasn't, 'Oh please, Vince, come back.' It was more like, 'Hey, asshole, you have more work to do here, you have reasons to come back and all the struggles that entails. Here's some of what you've done. Here's some of what we've done together, so you can at least connect.'

"It didn't seem like he responded much, but then I remember him kind of squirming. Some weeks later, he was able to start responding to nurses, pressure with the hand, squeezing once for yes. That kind of stuff."

Although I would remain semicomatose for several more weeks, on December 30 I began mouthing words.

Kathleen says, "During that first week it became a reality for me—we were in very serious trouble. I remember the first time I didn't get to go in to see Vince, I was heartbroken. I wanted to be there every minute because I wanted to see if there was any progress, what was going on. He could only have visitors a few times a day, and of course his family wanted to see him. So I sat some more and waited and waited, and the family was nice to me and gave me a chance to see him.

"He wouldn't come around. I wanted to know what could be done. I wanted to know if he could hear me. I wanted to know if he could move. I wanted to know everything. The nurses tried to explain brain injury to me. 'There are no facts, but from our experience, we believe that he can hear you, and the important thing now is that he needs to come around. He needs to regain consciousness.'

"They also explained that he'd had such a hard knock to the brain that the swelling was just humongous, that there was pressure everywhere, and that was going to be a long process. There was nothing more they could do. We just had to wait for the swelling to go down, and then they could see what had really been hurt and what hadn't. Their main emphasis was to try and get him to regain consciousness, wait for the swelling to go down, and keep him alive.

"When I first went in to see him, I was quiet and scared to touch him. Well, going in whining and crying and whispering was not getting us there, so I started whipping him around a little bit. Grabbing on him, pushing on him, and talking louder to him. The nurses were encouraging me, 'Talk to him, try to get him to come around.' That's when I had the idea about the tape: 'If you're going to live, then you can just get back to work. Take your pick: die or get back to work. This in-between stuff just isn't cutting it.' Or, 'Vince, come on, wake up, we've got to redo these vocals, man. Vince, come on, man, we gotta go redo these vocals. The recording's not finished yet.' That was all I could think of. That recording session was the biggest thing in his life. He had been so excited about it, and it was the last thing that had happened to him. Maybe it would trigger something. And he was trying and trying to come around. It just seemed like forever."

Tim Leatherwood says, "Vince was absolutely pale, and everything he did was in ultra slow motion. I found myself in the ICU screaming and yelling at him and barely getting him to roll his eyeballs and twitch a little bit, barely open an eye, and then he'd go back into the coma. I'm still amazed he was able to make the recovery back. And then not having any memory of it. To me the most tragic aspect about the whole thing, outside of the obvious, was that they had to cut his fucking vocal chord to do the tracheotomy."

In the midst of all the wagging tongues and crossed eyes of my friends, my smallish mother with her comfortable Southern accent came to my bedside and said, "Vince, this is your mother. Can you move your arm for your mother? Vince, this is your mother. Why don't you move your arm for your mother? Vince, can you move your arm for your mother?"

As the story goes, I slowly raised my left arm without opening my eyes and shot her the bird. She became tearfully exuberant, laughing and crying at the same time, and proceeded to fuss around the intensive-care floor telling everyone, "That's my Vince, he flipped me off! He's going to be just fine."

"The first time I went to visit Vince in ICU was about two weeks after the accident," says Bob Sturtevant. "There were a lot of other people in the waiting room who wanted to see him. Mandy Mercier and I went in together. Vince was still in the coma. I recall Mandy crying. She didn't say much."

Mandy Mercier was a young break-playing violinist from New York when I met her in Austin in the middle '70s. We had worked many of the same bars and clubs, and with so much in common had become good friends. Mandy never wasted the opportunity to help where she was needed. She made herself available to me now and again through the quiet years to follow. Mandy had only quality time to give.

Bob continues, "I tried to talk to Vince as though he were awake, because I felt like he was hearing what I was saying. I felt like there was a very subtle response. I could tell you were in there, you just weren't ready to come out yet. It would be one hell of a long time until I let you put a hammer in your hand.

"Just before Mandy and I went in, Shary told us about Vince's mother and a nurse trying to get Vince to do exercises—move his right hand and his left foot, and move his left hand and his right foot—and about his shooting her the bird. We knew that he might be asleep on the outside, but he was awake on the inside. It was a great relief."

On January 3, 1983, I had the operation to reconstruct my right arm.

NEUROLOGY CONSULTATION

The patient is semi-comatose, moves all extremities spontaneously in response to pain, but the left lower extremity less than the right lower extremity. There are multiple scalp lacerations. Exam of his ears demonstrates no evidence of basilar or skull fractures. Cranial nerves exam demonstrated an anisocoria; the left pupil is slightly larger than the right. The conjunctiva and the cornea on the right on the lower half are somewhat cloudy. His pupils do respond to light and accommodation. He does have doll's-eye movements. Corneal reflexes are weakly present bilaterally, and he does have weak lid reflexes. Motor facial function appears to be normal. An endotracheal tube is in place. Exam of motor power extremities demonstrates movement of all extremities, left lower extremity less than right lower extremity. He is spastic in the lower extremities. On DTRs, he is hyperreflexic in the lower extremities, he has bilateral Babinskis, and he has unsustained ankle clonus bilaterally. Cerebeller exam could not be performed. CT scan is reviewed and was felt to be within normal limits, except for slight effacement of the right lateral ventricle.

Impression: Traumatic encephalopathy secondary to closed-head injury.

Recommendations: From my standpoint, there are no recommendations other than supportive care and restriction of fluid intake to prevent cerebral edema. An ophthalmological consult is suggested because of clouding of the right conjunctiva. Will follow patient.

Mandy, who had been visiting regularly, says, "As Vince began to come out of the coma, I remember him turning his head and his eyes looking right at me and then just continuing to move, without stopping. He was apparently conscious, he was awake, but there was no difference in his expressions between my face and the wall—it was like a radar beam or searchlight just going across my face. It scared the hell out of me because—who is in there? Who's left? What is this? I'd never seen anything like that."

♪ *XV* ♪

Room 933

*O*n January 8, I began to write, left-handed
in a scrawl, on a yellow legal pad that I still have:

> Drink Water. No people. Goodbye.
> I just want something wet.
> Help get my head up.
> Tom Pacheco.
> Oxygen.
> Juice. Turn off the fan.
> Suction.
> I'm tired but I'll do what you ask. Let me have some Coke to
> drink.
> I'm tired.

On January 9, I was transferred out of the ICU to Room 933. Letters and cards that survive include:

> Vince—
>   You picked a hell of a way to quit smoking. We didn't want
> to wake you, but anybody that sleeps for two weeks deserves
> to be woken up. Glad you're back with us, you were a long
> way out there.
>   Hang in there,
>   Earl

I love Vince. Me too. You were asleep. Nice room! Catch ya next time.

Stephen and Franci

Dear Vinco,

I was so sorry to hear about your accident. We are all so glad to hear that you are on the road to recovery. Do what the doctors tell you.

Joy

Western Union Telegram
Alexandria, Virginia

Vince, get off your ass. We love you and are talking to God and anyone else who will listen and get you well. Do what the doctors tell you unless it's unethical.

Much love and more later,

Lucinda, Clyde, and Hobart

Dear Vince,

Knowing that wishes have power, take heart! All will be well.

Providence and Donn Billings

Dear Vince,

Was very distressed to hear of the accident. I sincerely hope you are bearing up well under it all. I know how really awful it can get sometimes when it feels like you've lost so much. I know there just isn't much anyone can say. You were a really good friend to us when we needed it, would like to think we could return it. Don't know if there's anything we can do from this distance, but we're here and extend whatever support we can.

May peace return.

Joanie

Dear Vince,

We were both shocked and sad to hear about your accident. Being so far away makes it even worse. There's not much we can do except hope and pray for your full recovery.

We sorely miss Vinco music. Our collection of Vince Bell music on tape has impressed our friends, but the tapes are wearing thin from use. Must get back to Texas to refill my supply.

Can never forget the good times you gave us—the inspired madness at the Fair for the "Christmas Song" before you left for Tahoe, the joy of your return to Houston and the KPFT benefit with songs about your trip, opening night at Sweetheart of Texas Concert Hall and Saloon, a night at the Old Quarter (20 degrees outside, 21 degrees inside), froze our asses off and sang harmony, the Level Flight Band, more madness at Liberty Hall.

If we can be of any help just let us know. We're far away, but have many friends in Texas for support. God bless you, get back Vince.

With love,

John and Kathi Lopez

P.S. Enclosed is a photo to help you remember who the heck we are.

Vince,

We came by but missed you. A few smokes to tide you over. See you soon.

Love,

Stephen and Franci

Kathleen Vick came to see me every day. "It was a very big day when Vince got out of intensive care. He had a therapist, kind of his compadre, who was there all the time teaching Vince to feed himself. Vince had to completely start from the beginning. I thought this would be a big breakthrough, but I realized at that point that it had just begun. His surviving the wreck and getting out of intensive care was not the relief, not the, 'Oh well, it's done now. All we have to do is wait a little bit and he'll be back to normal.' That didn't happen. It was never going to happen. The real work began then for him.

"Only after he regained consciousness and was taken off the machines and put in his own room did he start asking himself, Who am I? What am I? What's going on? How did this happen? What do I have to do? Why can't I do what I think I should be able to do? The hard part really started then.

"The therapist told me that Vince was too dependent on me. I wanted to protect him. I didn't want anybody pushing him. But that's when they wanted to push him the hardest. That's when they had to be the strictest. He was childlike because he was having a hard time remembering anything. A lot of his short-term memory was missing, and he was very confused. And he was angry, but he didn't know who to be angry at, or what to be angry about. That side of Vince was there almost all the time, but it wasn't tempered with reason, so it was really hard to take."

My first memories are of pressing the nurses' button for shots of painkiller. I would ring them often, and I would ring them early. Though I was barely cognizant, I was intensely aware if the shots were late because of the terrific pain. I needed those shots. That was all. Life was injection to injection, and I depended on them. My rebuilt right arm was hurting horribly. I was no longer a songwriter, a musician, a wage-earner or a capable person of any kind. What I knew or could recall would fill a thimble, maybe.

I also have hazy recollections of trying to walk alone. Anywhere, but firstly to the toilet in my hospital room. One foot after the other. Half staggering, with half the hair shaved off my head. Dried blood on my gown, right arm in a sling. The next numbing thud was my skull resounding off the tiles somewhere beneath the sink. I could barely balance myself, much less walk, so getting up off that floor was some journey. When I returned to lie in that tall bed, I was uncertain and disoriented. Then I called a nurse for another shot.

✦ ✦ ✦

"One evening I went to the hospital to visit," tells Mandy. "It was dark out. Vince didn't know who I was, but he knew I was a friend. There was sort of a little-boy quality to him then. He was talking about a monster, some kind of a big monster that almost got him, but didn't get him. I said, 'That monster's not going to come back, it's okay.' Just talking to him. He went into the bathroom, which he could just do by himself by then. He had hospital pants on, and he asked me to tie the string for him. It was a bow. 'Is that all right? It's not too tight?' It was so moving."

After you get tagged that hard, you get simple. Not much bothers you for long. I stumbled around like a spectator in the weeks that followed, giving looks that were frozen, vacant. Nobody talked to me. I was so spacey, I couldn't have responded if I had wanted to. I would hobble jerkily around, childlike, meeting other patients the nurses wanted me to meet. They treated me understandingly. I welcomed the odd sense of pity and warmed to some, but my difficulty with walking and talking took its toll. I blankly wanted to be wheeled to the window that faced out onto Interstate 35, nine floors above the highway where my accident had occurred.

My purposeful condition must have looked to the other patients and hospital staff like courage. The confusing fact was that I could look nowhere for an example of how to claw and crawl through this unbelievably bizarre reality in which I found myself.

"So, Vince was out of the intensive care situation and I was backing off a little," confides Kathleen. "Bill Browder was visiting then along other friends, and that seemed to be what the hospital staff wanted—more people to visit and help him recollect, and the family influence.

"I went up one day, and he was struggling to feed himself. The therapist was there with him, but it was just hard. Vince had on a hospital gown—it looked like something out of the movie *One Flew Over the Cuckoo's Nest*. He was sitting there in a split-open gown. So I zipped down to a surplus store and got him three pairs of jogging shorts and some T-shirts so the man could be dressed. Vince is so proud. It was the indignity of it that I couldn't stand, because I respected him so much. He's such a proud man."

When my younger brother Gary came to visit, he found a dazed-looking man in a stained, green hospital gown fumbling in front of the Coke machine. He felt sorry for the poor fellow with half a head of hair and an arm webbed like a tennis racket trying to negotiate quarters into the tiny slice of a coin box. He looked really hard but didn't recognize me. My skin was "gray like a shark," he told me later.

I was desperately grasping at phantoms of the heart. After my brother left, I searched for the only healthy-acting patient I had taken a liking to. An attendant told me that he had gone. That was hard to comprehend from my incomplete patchwork of consciousness. I wandered tentatively, forgetfully, into the hall several times to look for him. A nurse finally cradled me by my good arm as I breathlessly complained, "I just wanted to talk to him."

She nodded, slowly herding me back toward my room, "There, there, honey, he died of something exotic." Those words mocked me through that night. This was utterly impossible. He was strong as an ox. And he laughed. He almost made me laugh once. Someone needed to save the day. I was sitting up in my bed in the half-light of a murmuring television with the remote control in my senseless, dyslexic hand. I rocked back and forth as I whimpered to myself again and again in low, barely audible tones, "Someone needs to save the day."

From out of nowhere someone did.

I started to be a "traumatic brain injury survivor." A husband and wife team of occupational therapists, what they call OTs in medical lingo, were my attendants. They wanted pure and simple the best for me. I've always thought of them as inspiring my quick start at rehabilitating myself. They would reassuringly coax me from bed and then wheel me past galleries of queer lights, buzzers, and bells to the elevator and down to the fifth floor to exercise. I could barely crutch my legs past those gleaming jogging-machines. My voice refused to talk above a transparent whistle and wheeze. I would stare and drool. They would sit me down and put my ravaged right hand into a two-gallon jug filled with pebbles, as they coaxed, "Can you feel the penny, Vince? Can you pick up the penny?"

♪   *XVI*   ♪

If It Was Time for the Musicians to Call, It Was Time to Go Home and Fix It

*T*he fellow who ran into me with a Ford LTD was fined $600 for ending my life. In one split second he threw my chosen career to the dogs. He put me into an uncertain loop of treatment after treatment for many years to come.

"A day or two after the accident I had gone to the police station to talk to an investigator about the kid who had been driving the car," Shary remembers. "I asked what they were going to do to this dude—what kind of charges were they going to file? What was going to happen to this guy who's screwed my brother up so badly? The investigator said, 'Well, we can't charge him with anything now.' I just about came unglued.

"They were still waiting to see if Vince lived or died. If they filed a lesser charge immediately and then Vince died, they wouldn't be able to re-file new charges. There was also a lot of confusion about exactly what had happened. The car was registered to someone who hadn't been in the car. The driver was the owner's nephew or son.

81

And they had a hard time determining the driver's nationality; he wasn't a U.S. citizen.

"The four or five people in the other car were taken to the hospital, too—treated and released for minor cuts and bruises. It was just a carload of young people out driving drunk. The officer said that from all the damage to the car, and from what they did know about the accident, that they were traveling about 70 miles an hour when they broadsided Vince."

Shary grimaces. "I saw the car. There was an imprint of Vince's head above the top of the door jamb, and this was a '64 Ford Fairlane—a steel tank. You could see why Vince was damaged so badly, because in the process of flying out of the car he smacked his head and got a four-inch-long indention in the side of his skull.

"The police finally did file charges, but they didn't even charge him with drunk driving. I was told that the police at the scene felt sorry for him and waited before they gave him a breathalyzer. In the end, he was fined $600. I was so mad when the cop told me that. Back then you didn't have to have citizenship to be able to get a driver's license in the state of Texas. You could be illegal as hell, but you could go down to get a driver's license, no problem.

"So, they fined him $600, and that was it."

"My advice for those who die," like the line from the Beatles song says, was to pick my challenges deftly. I hadn't time for indignation, anger, or ill will. No grudges would help. I could tell that even this early on, from the strange and unfamiliar depths from which I was gloomily peering. It would take the best of my thoughts, the bravest of my intentions, plus tedious years of toil just to relearn how to do the simple things. The path of malice and animosity had always pointed straight downhill. That would only take precious time from me—time I didn't have. I would find that time and patience were now my biggest allies.

My father said that the fellow who destroyed me and that powder-blue Ford Fairlane was from a chronically poor east Austin family. Suing him for my pains would be unrealistic and, practically speaking, pointless. Dad closed his conversation with me by saying, "You feel like stabbing a man when he's down, Vince?"

I said somewhat resignedly, "No, sir."

Knowing how awkward I felt, Dad added, "You need to learn how to turn around, walk, and whistle. Starting today wouldn't be too soon."

I followed him as closely as the skin crawling up my nerve-damaged arms. From then on, I would try to envision that I had run into a tree in my car. It wasn't easy to do, but with the years of pain and the re-learning, I didn't need the resentment that blaming someone else for my troubles would entail. This was a struggle from the outset. It didn't hurt that I couldn't remember anything at all for a while.

It took a lot to leave my room at first. If I didn't understand a thing about my life, I at least knew Room 933. And that room was the only place I knew. It was my home. There were haunting, unanswerable questions like Who was I? What did I do? Where did I live? Where was I going? Lying in the hospital bed in Room 933, I would find that I had left most of 32 busy years on the bumper of an LTD.

A carpet of short hair was growing on the bald side of my head. I was still very dazed. I was clueless, a dim little bulb. Friends visited, but I didn't have the foggiest who they were. Once reminded, I could recognize them from there on out. People didn't mean much. When you are an amputee, they take your arms and legs. When you are head-injured, they take your thoughts. Tomorrow offered, most dolefully, not a glimmer of hope.

Nor could any of my attending physicians be sure of how badly I was damaged. It was impossible still to discern what body parts were all right and what was horribly wrong. I couldn't reach my hands above my head. The pains were intense.

There would be a universe worth of problems after that, but it was still too early to even have problems. I was desperate to do anything that would make me feel somewhat "normal" like everyone else I saw, even if for just a moment. I wanted to envision myself halfway whole again, yet I no longer recognized that faraway place. That made my drive to redevelop myself all-consuming yet somehow completely inadequate when compared to the task.

I vaguely remember being very calm, very resolute, committed, and confident in the face of the monolithic. Like a man facing oblivion, I feared no one, no thing. I knew the value to a person like me of the adversarial, so I toughed up in my shattered private thoughts. This head injury dude, he's one big son of a bitch. But he's got no business fucking with me.

No one, from the neuroscientist who brought me back to life to the physical therapists who saw me every week, could tell what lay ahead. I remember pleading desperately, in my stuttering whisper, with one of my many doctors, "Will I ever w-w-walk or t-t-talk again?"

"I don't know," the doctor replied helplessly. "You'll have to tell us."

While I stared silently out the window of the hospital room, it would feel far more hopeful, logical, and appealing to be like a rock or a tree. I needed help, nobody knew that better.

On January 18 I checked myself into a hospital across town on the advice of an attending physician. He pumped up the place to me, saying their facilities for brain injury were the best, so I reluctantly made the change. Later I discovered that he was on the payroll at this hospital. His seemingly earnest advice for me to change facilities in midstream would appear thereafter insincere and mercenary. But as I said, I didn't have time for that now.

Bob Sturtevant again paints the picture: "The first time I went to see Vince in the new hospital, he was sitting in a common room and there were other people in the room. Vince was sitting in a wheelchair unattended. He began wafting his right hand, shaking his hand, as though to get circulation in it. He was constantly moving that hand to get it to wake up, I guess. He was deeply damaged. His head was shaved and still swollen. He looked up at me and recognized me immediately because I had visited often at Brackenridge. I squatted down, and we visited for ten minutes. He was aware of where he was, but he was really slowed down, terribly hurt. I asked him if there was anything he needed. I asked him how he was. I touched him, put my arms around him. It was obvious in his eyes, in his demeanor, that it was going to be a long road back.

"Then I heard that Vince was not satisfied with his physical therapy, that he was not a happy camper. One of the things that really got to him there was that they kept trying to 'assimilate' him into the larger population. I think he just wanted to eat by himself."

"It was a shock to me that he left Brackenridge," Kathleen says. "He was in a room with bare walls and a mattress on the floor. That's all he was given. It was like he was in prison. I was furious. I go to see him there for the first time and it's the nut floor—what the hell is this? At first they didn't want me to see him. I was brazen and raised such hell that they took me in, and there he was, beside himself because he wasn't crazy. He knew what was going on. He just had trouble communicating. He was extremely upset by this.

"This was one of the very worst days I remember throughout the whole ordeal. I was quivering, I was so furious, and I was so hurt for him. He told me that they wouldn't let him eat alone. He was helpless to do anything about it. It was just horrible that they would put him where everybody was mentally ill, when the man had a brain injury. They wanted to institutionalize him with a bunch of people that didn't have the same problems he had. I thought he'd be in some kind of therapy where they understood the problem, instead of treating him like a child who wouldn't behave. It wasn't a question of acting right. He wasn't ill, he wasn't retarded, he wasn't a child, and he wasn't antisocial.

"He was sitting on the corner of a mattress, and I sat there with him and tried to calm him down. I told him we'd do something. I couldn't get him out, of course, and if I made too much trouble they weren't going to let me out, either," Kathleen laughs. "He was more upset there than anywhere else, or at any other time."

As was brutally obvious, I wasn't made comfortable by the new institution. I was self-conscious about my new condition of less than a month. I just wanted to eat in my room. But because I didn't want to drool and stutter over hot dogs in their cafeteria, they said, "We think you're antisocial, Mr. Bell."

I said, "I think you're fired," and was outta there, in an ambulance, before lunch that day. That was the first time I ever fired a hospital. And it didn't feel so bad. That taught me the unenviably tough lesson that my recovery was far too complex and important to leave up to the professionals. Though I was groping in a dense fog, I could tell that some of us were only here to make a living while some of us were here perhaps to live again. Early on, I was determined that the people whose only stake in my rehabilitation was a paycheck would not get it.

I realized at the same time, however, that though I would have to accomplish my goals in my own way, I had to do it without losing one thread of sorely needed help. I had to manage my own renaissance but without sacrificing any assistance from others. Help could come from anywhere in this rough old world that I would let it. As independent as I figured I had to be, I still had to acknowledge that all the solutions would not come from within. Maybe I was too proud and too headstrong, but I was not there to be denied. A song I had written put it this way, "I'm taking the long way to heaven, ain't nobody knows it better than me."

I've always felt that the contentious side of me is one of my better sides. I've certainly misused it from time to time, and it has sometimes been misunderstood by others, but it's probably why I'm standing today. Or still standing. And you bet, I was damn well difficult. Sometimes I was my own worst advisor.

On January 24, 1983, I checked back into Brackenridge.

Then a phone call from Stevie Ray Vaughan and Ray Wylie Hubbard, from one of the several benefit concerts being given for me around Texas, helped me leave all hospitals for good to go home. The money netted by all those benefit shows on my behalf paid all my bills for the first six months of 1983. I thought to myself, *If these musical folks who can't afford it are going to bail me out, I'll be damned if I'm gonna lie here and be helpless. If it was time for the musicians to call, it was time to go home and fix it.*

"We had a benefit at Anderson Fair," remembers Tim Leatherwood. "Nanci Griffith played, Lyle Lovett played, and Don Sanders. There might have been a few others in there. I think we sent him something like $1,200."

Kathleen recalls, "The *Austin Chronicle* and Joe Nick Patoski wrote some big stories about Vince, the accident, and the benefit concerts. Eddie Wilson at Threadgill's gave $1000, and the Continental Club made a donation. We had the biggest benefit at Steamboat Springs on Sixth Street. It was an all-star event. Riverside Recording Studio, where we had been recording, provided the sound system. Everybody was there, and we taped it. Stevie, Eric, and all the people that had been working with Vince on the recordings showed up. Ray Hubbard. I think even Jerry Jeff Walker was there.

"After the benefits, Vince decided that if he were going to get better, it was really kind of up to him. And, of course, Vince is real quick to—well, you'd show him something and he'd think he could do it. 'I don't need this person, or that person.' He was always self-diagnosis, self-therapy, self-everything. Which was what he ended up doing.

"But the years after that were just tough. It took a long time. It was the beginning of a long, hard road—what's that song he wrote?" Shary soberly quotes a verse from one of the songs I had written in the '70s. "'It's a tough row to hoe, it's blistering cold. The lights go low and the story gets told. Your eyes close slowly, telling me you understand.'"

♪ *XVII* ♪

Providence Street

I was released from Brackenridge County Hospital on February 3, 1983.

A couple of months of hospitalization did not prepare me for the flood of disappointments I would endure when I returned to my home. I couldn't stay awake, so I didn't leave the bed much. Memories of everyday life and of my dearest friends were either erased completely or bewilderingly abbreviated. It was way beyond my ability to understand the depth of my injuries or how it would affect every one of my relationships. Though it may sound selfish, I was consumed with my own unanswerable questions. Would I ever walk like before? Would I talk, taste, feel my arms and legs, much less play music and resume my career? If so, how?

"Both Vince and Melody were in therapy after they got home," says Bob Sturtevant. "Each of them was in a different world, almost as though they were living in separate houses. It felt like a house of anguish."

Kathleen appraised the situation, "Once Vince and Melody got back to the house, they just didn't know each other anymore. They were both in their own private pain, their own private worlds."

✦ ✦ ✦

Shary says, "Vince was awake, but you really couldn't talk to him. His eyes were dilated. One minute he would be sitting there awake, and you would talk with him. He could talk back, but it was barely above a whisper, and he didn't have full breathing. He was really slow. He'd be talking to you and just fall out, asleep. I mean just off and on, like narcolepsy. He was like that for a long time."

My mother used to call that house on Providence "the doll house." I bought it because it was a huge parcel of property in a part of town where no one else wanted to live. It cost less than two new cars and looked like a place a writer could afford. The house was a shiplap frame construction of pier and beam. Built around the time I was born, it had enough wood in it to make three houses in 1980. The yard was a fifth of an acre, with a fence and a gravel driveway. It sat on a grassy hill overlooking Austin, at the confluence of the interstate and Texas Highway 290 to Houston.

The house was in a loose neighborhood of me and some old black men and women. We had all worked to own the clapboard homes and mobile trailers we lived in. But we were all out of the flow of the locale, just barely hanging on to that American dream. It appeared like wind-whipped, black dirt, Central Texas plains. The grass waved knee-high in the wind, with pop bottles, gum wrappers, and faded plastic hamburger trays half-buried in the sticky black soil. It grew wildly long at the street corners around the occasional fire plug. An elementary school stood abandoned on the hill, with rows of cloudy glass windows like broken teeth in the whistling wind.

From where I would dream of rekindling my life, you could hear the tire-tread singing roadways. Jet plane tarmacs at the old airport resounded like kettle drums a couple of miles distant. All day and night. The world passed along here, or stopped to buy a tank of gas, or a night in a motel room, or a plastic swimming pool for the kids.

On one side of my little brown house was Ira. He worked daily. His yard was crammed full of salvage. Some he used in his contracting jobs. There were several piles of brick and cinder blocks. Bales of wire, old rusting lawn mowers, torn bags of cement, and parts of an Oldsmobile of some ancient variety were littered about. An old wooden garage was falling down. Stacks of boards with big black spiders in them and flowering weeds up to your head leaned in between. Two junkyard dogs had the run of the place. Their trails would snake along the fence next door to my tiny 800-square foot writer's home.

On the other side was a sparrow-boned woman named Mary, who lived in a two-room shack 12-feet long, maybe 7-feet deep. She was neat as a pin, old as the hills, and seemed to live on nothing at all. She still gardened some of what she ate in her fenceless backyard. She walked everywhere, which was mostly to a ramshackle white church a block over. She was always pleasant, speaking infrequently and with great calm in her voice. There must have been half a century between us. I don't think she had a TV set. We smiled and waved every time we saw one another.

When I started out that spring of 1983, I couldn't rest my hands on my hips because of the pain. In the midst of all the mental and neural reprogramming that was going on, I physically hurt very badly. Every day I taped the electrodes of a battery-powered electronic unit to my right arm. It would shock me every few seconds to control my suffering. I had to keep handwritten directions for how to use the "Tens" unit tacked to a wall so I wouldn't forget them.

I was also extremely simplified, and very emotional. People would come over to talk. I was so confused that if they offered to go to the store to replenish my supplies, I would cry because I thought they were deserting me. It was so hard for anyone besides me to see how much of the tapes in my brain were erased. My speech was very slow, quiet, hoarse. I was really dim, really simple, really sweet, and really appreciative of life around the very few people I seemed to know.

Mandy Mercier remembers, "This was a very needy phase. Vince would want you to stay longer, or maybe cry if you left. But his need was so infinite that you felt, *What the hell can I do?* If it helps a little to come over, sure, but you can't be there all the time. I always had the feeling that Vince was still there but that his radio dial had moved a little bit off the station. But he was always still Vince—and if he could figure out how, he could bring Vince back. The basic premise of the head injury mythology is that it's a great tragedy, and that it's an irrevocable thing. 'You might get better, but don't count on it.' I remember thinking first that it was a tragedy because this was such a brilliant person, and then thinking, *He's so brilliant that he can probably figure this out; it's just a matter of time.*"

"A lot of the time he was just quiet," my sister Shary says. "You didn't know what he was thinking. It was like someone in a daze, or as if he was daydreaming. And he would sleep a lot; he did need a lot of rest."

"As bits of memory started flying back through his head, he would have part of one thing from one point in time, and part of one from another," explained Kathleen Vick. "They would come together in his mind. Unless you knew everything that he was pulling together, as more and more things started to return to him, you just lost track. It was like walking into a monologue in the middle of a movie. Who's that? What's that?

"It took a long time for Vince to even figure out where he had left off, exactly. He had to put that all into perspective and figure out where he'd been, and then what point he was at now. You go through something like he did and you change, or what you want to do sometimes changes drastically."

"I began spending a lot of time with Vince when he got back home," Bob Sturtevant says. "For many months I did projects around the house—remodeling the interior a little bit or other jobs. One day Marion and I got there, and Vince was shaking his hand—that activity went on for quite a long while. He was also drooling, and Marion saw it. He saw her see him and said, 'Excuse me, that's a bad habit I picked up at the hospital.'

"Vince always wanted to get involved in whatever I was doing. He always wanted to help out. He had been that way before the wreck. The world's best helper. Now, he still wanted to do things but physically just wasn't capable of doing very much. But he'd be there if I needed a hammer, if I needed a this or a that.

"One day I went out and bought a screwdriver for him that had a round knob handle, because he didn't have any strength in his right hand. He could take that screwdriver and actually turn screws, so I could give him a few jobs that he could do. And he did them, too. He would just sit there and sweat—it was getting into the summertime—but he was very determined."

Bill Browder says, "I remember Vince's struggles to walk and just to do the little things that we take for granted. He couldn't move his arm a certain way, or get his fingers to do certain things that he used to be able to do. And not just fingers and arms, but legs, brain, everything. It was a very long, agonizing rehabilitation."

My mother recalled Bill from those dark days as "that nice boy who was always there." When she had arrived at my hospital bed from Michigan, Bill went to the store to buy her the tennis shoes she wore while pacing the intensive care ward. "When Vince came outside on the porch I'd have to help him down the stairs," Bill says, "or back up them. It was bleak. I didn't think he would come back. I didn't write him off, but to say that the effect was pretty pronounced is an understatement. He was making a go of it, but those were pretty dark days."

Lagging abilities seemed to be everywhere now. But I found that what was denied me could be outflanked. In other words, if I couldn't write comfortably or well with a pen anymore, then I could type. In that dizzy, unfamiliar year, typing was the way to tomorrow. With everything, if I would just take my time and do the hard thinking first, I could figure a new way. I could count on my thoughts to be resourceful, to help me find different paths in this world so that I could be just like all the "normal" people. I was sluggishly learning to adapt.

"I think that was the frustrating part for him," Kathleen agrees. "Just getting his mind to show him beginnings, middles, and ends. He couldn't see the process. That was a frustrating time, too, because as more things were coming back to him, and he saw more people, the more he got a sense of what he had been capable of doing in comparison to what he was capable of now. He began to get a picture of what his life had been. The concept that he couldn't just go from here to there was hard for him.

"Even the simplest things that he wanted to do were, 'No, you can't do that.' 'No, you can't go here,' or 'No, it's too early for that.' It genuinely surprised him that whatever he wanted to do, he couldn't do. Once it entered his mind, he expected that he would be able to. He just never seemed to accept the hardcore reality that his brain had been beaten up and it was going to be a while. He never seemed to grasp that he was going to have to learn all this from scratch.

"That reaction came and went pretty quickly, and then he would think, 'Well okay, where do I have to start?' If you could give him a starting point, no matter how far back, he could start working hard at it. But until he could see the avenue, it would be, 'I want to play guitar.' 'Well, you can't.' The 'you can't' was unacceptable. So it had to be, 'You can't because your arm's all screwed up. You can listen to tapes. You can pick it up and learn how to hold it. You can figure out if you're left-handed or right-handed.' You had to help him find a starting point to do anything, and then that was okay. It didn't matter how hard it was, if he could just find the starting point."

Often I'd end up sitting in the window, just as I had in the hospital, and typing images, not in an organized conversational form at all but rather like a private revealing. I hung onto ideas like they were precious. They were so elusive because I couldn't remember much from moment to moment. This stream-of-consciousness reporting in the typewritten pages underscored how desperately scattered my thoughts were. However, they pointed up at least a healthy curiosity despite the handicaps.

> IT CAME UP LIKE A HURRICANE, TOOK EVERYTHING.
> THE PLACES I HELD SO DEAR ARE GONE.
> LAUGHTER THAT FILLED THE AIR IS JUST A MEMORY.
> MOMENTS I GLADLY SHARED FOR A SONG.

I had showed up on my own doorstep like a pup with two broken paws. Dan Earhart, that first piano player of mine, said he didn't think I could walk into a grocery and buy something then, because I wasn't remembering or recognizing much. My nervous system was a mess. My vantage point had certainly changed since being in a downtown hospital, but most things were dreadfully the same now, only a lot more quiet. I sent the posse out to find that brain injury bastard, only to find him under my nails. I consoled myself, *You know, there's a race every day. Somewhere. So what if you can't show up at the contest today to get your cup of gratification. Don't worry. There's a race tomorrow.*

> THIS ATMOSPHERE IS MORE CONDUCIVE TO
> PULLING RABBITS OUT OF YOUR HAT.

ICE CREAM, TV CONTROL.
... TO THE WINDOW TO SIT IN THE CHAIR.

I lived a long way down the road from the rest of the world. But I knew that I couldn't afford the luxury of pessimism. Every few hours was a cheerleading session about what I had been able to accomplish in the minutes before. I was remarkably positive, according to friends. I had to work at keeping my spirits up when the accomplishments were as basic as gripping a ball or recognizing the pictures on the walls of my house. "Has that always been there?" I asked about the *Bermuda Triangle* ballet poster that had been hanging there since 1980. That inability to recall has never gone away. The methods and tricks I developed to combat the condition only make it seem as if it has.

Since I couldn't remember much about anything, I transcribed impressions constantly. NO ONE CAN KNOCK THE SONG OUT OF ME, I would type. I believed that what I had been through already would allow me to get through whatever came next, and that patience would see me through. I pursued the quiet victories with passion. Where I could work without comparison and out from under convention was where I thought I ought to be.

 I AM MOST COMFORTABLE WHEN STRAINING AT THE
   BIT.
PERFORM OR PERISH.
LET THAT FRIDAY THE THIRTEENTH GUY IN HERE,
   I'LL SCARE THE HELL OUT OF HIM.
WATCHING THE RAIN GAUGE IS ONE OF MY FUN
   THINGS TO DO HERE.
FIVE MONTHS AFTER THE WRECK, I DROVE MYSELF
   UNASSISTED.
I'M LUCKY TO BE ALIVE.

Shary says, "Vince took the van out a few times and I was worried to death that he was going to have another accident. He shouldn't have been behind the wheel. He still had no balance, and we were worried about his falling. He talked really slowly. Not very much breath. Very soft. Like slow motion. His eyes were still dilated all the time. He had to move very slowly. We didn't want him to fall and hit his head or hurt his arm. People would get on either side of him, hold his arms, and walk with him to keep him going straight.

"One night a couple of us took him to a Chinese restaurant. Vince began talking more and more slowly and then just got quiet. When the waitress asked if she could get us anything, Vince went down face-first into his soup. He just fell asleep, right there at the table in the restaurant. Then he woke up. It was a constant thing—awake 15 minutes, out 5 minutes, awake 30 minutes. I thought he was doing well to stay awake for an hour and a half at a time."

I was never coerced by my family, but instead they supported me steadily and still do. Though they were the closest people to me, they understood precious little of the bizarre view from the broken little windows of my mind.

My sister, Lana, says about those early days, "I think our father thought that whatever chance Vince had for a career in music was over. Nobody knew, especially with a head injury, if he would ever be anything more than what he was right out of the hospital. Dad felt that Vince would need some kind of intensive care for the rest of his life—it was serious enough for him to tell me that he thought it was all over."

While squeezing a tennis ball, I would roust from bed to make jerking treks to the typewriter to put down the thoughts that constantly assailed me. This was before I could write with my rebuilt right arm. I typed everything in capital letters because, when everything was double-spaced and capitalized, I could see it better. My eye coordination was very bad. It was hard to read, with the letter forms drifting sometimes upside down or backward on the page. By typing every-thing all caps, I more clearly had someone to relate to daily, even if it was only an Italian portable. I could share the burden with someone who didn't talk much.

> YOU ARE DUMBER THAN OTHER PEOPLE. YOU MUST
>   GO SLOWER.
> HERE IS A TIP TO YESTERDAY, AND WE SURVIVORS
>   WHO GOT AWAY.
> DON'T CRY, YOU'RE ON THE DIFFICULT WAY BACK.

Words would continue to drift around the page all during 1983 and 1984. That had something to do with the severe dyslexia in the entire left side of my body. The condition showed itself in the first doctor's observations of the left leg, back in the comatose days at Bracken-ridge. My brain was failing to get the signals to my body uniformly, and that left a distinct lag in my step.

It seemed one side of me no longer talked to the other side. I told people, "The right arm was destroyed. The left arm was over in the corner asleep." I walked like a clubfoot, with a stagger I couldn't shake. This extended into my stomach and arm muscles. It took years for me to even recognize exactly what the problem was, and then learn to control it. The vigilance I kept up ultimately allowed me to function smoothly in my body.

I tried to take care of the little things. The big things would have to take care of themselves. The more impossible the task, the harder I tried to break down its huge impossibilities into smaller increments. This technique would help me turn a thousand complex situations into the simple and manageable. First light every day brought a new pot of coffee, good thoughts, and double spaces on my buddy the typewriter.

In the vaguest early days of 1983, I would lie in bed, look down at my feet, and strive to make the left toes bend and point like the right ones, not bind like stone into strange attitudes. I wore out the tops of many pairs of shoes for years to come because my left big toe stuck straight up uncontrollably.

I would also attempt to stand while shifting my weight from the heel to toe. It would take my best balance to keep from falling over. I sometimes crashed horribly while gingerly standing in place next to my bed. The electronic unit dangled around my neck while wired to my arm, shocking me every eight seconds.

> COUNT ONE, AND TWO, AND THREE, AND FOUR...
>   ON THE TRAMPOLINE.
> FALLING ON YOUR FACE IS THE INEVITABLE FIRST
>   STEP TOWARD SUCCESS.
> YOU MAY HAVE SEEN SOMEONE TRAVEL A MORE
>   CIRCUITOUS ROUTE, BUT YOU'VE NEVER SEEN
>   ANYONE COME ANY FARTHER.
> I'M IN IT FOR THE LONG HAUL.
> I AM SPENDING MONTHS OF TIME LEARNING YEARS'
>   WORTH OF WORK, BIT BY BLEEDING BIT.
> HIS ABILITY TO HEEL AND TOE ON HIS LEFT SIDE IS
>   GONE. FIND IT. HEEL AND TOE IN THE MIRROR OF
>   THE WARDROBE. SEE WHAT THE HELL IS GOING ON.

Later that year, I would try to run in place, counting all the left footfalls out loud. This therapy was designed to work on my voice as much as the coordination in my legs. Most days I would jog, counting into the tens of thousands. This was the lonely routine every day for years to come. I was so uncoordinated. Running in place and counting proved to be the most difficult, challenging, and important exercises I did. Then I got a $30 jogging trampoline to continue. That saved my knees and ankles.

The concept of the "quiet victory" was born then. I would try to string together uncountable, anonymous conquests over deep disability, and no one would notice the progress but me. After I did relearn something—like how to pronounce a word—it was as if I'd never forgotten how to do it, because my memory was so bad. Those were days without end, nights without reason. But I knew full well that where my heart was, my fortune lay. I went to the mailbox for the first time then and was very excited about walking down the driveway.

Sometimes I didn't want to do anything, though. The enthusiast in me gave up. A feeling of so near and yet so far engulfed me. Sometimes I just didn't know what to do next. I felt like a leaf in the wind.

My ability to taste was gone for several years. The loss of taste and the numbness in my mouth made me lose bits of food, and I gagged often. I could also drown in a glass of water. It was years later that I learned how complicated swallowing is. Brain injury usually affects the ability to coordinate the nerves and 20-plus muscles in the neck and esophagus that are used to swallow. It was far more gratifying to pursue those preposterous little quiet victories. Eating became one of my least favorite things to do. I would weigh in at 130 pounds for a while.

> I ATE A DOLLAR AND NINETEEN CENTS' WORTH OF
>   FUDGE DROPS THIS WEEK.
> I MISS BEING ABLE TO TASTE. SO THIS IS THE WORLD
>   OF THE UNDEAD, HUH?
> THEY SAVED THE WRONG PERSON, I DON'T WANT TO
>   DO ANYTHING.
> GET USED TO QUIET VICTORIES, THEY'RE VICTORIES
>   NONETHELESS.

Then one day I could vaguely taste the sweetness in a drink. I was thrilled to become a sugar addict. Sugar on everything. I thought the sugar would rot the teeth out of my head until I discovered sweetener. Then it was sweetener with everything. Hamburgers, fries, salsas, chips, steaks, Tex-Mex, fish, fowl, they all were washed down with quantities of Kool-Aid, or iced tea, or Coke. But usually coffee. Coffee with four packets of sweetener helped me to stay awake during the days when I could barely stumble around for an hour without falling back into the bed exhausted.

"There was the ever-present Cuban coffee. He liked drinking that Bustello," says Bob Sturtevant. "He always liked coffee with a whang to it, and he'd make it stout enough to stand up on its hind legs. Later in the year he could take care of himself to a certain degree. He could walk somewhat at that point. He wasn't falling asleep all the time, though he needed to sleep a lot. The dilation in his eyes had receded by then—his eyes were almost back to normal. He still was very slow in speech, unless he was agitated or very angry. Even then, he wasn't fast by any means."

My daily schedule was inconsistent hour by hour for month after month. It was that way at night as well. I would often find myself staring out the window over my typewriter at the radio towers winking in small dots of red at four in the morning. I watched many a sunrise as the dawn would come over the backyard. Getting back to a workable schedule of any kind was one of the tasks I could look to no one for advice about. This would take most of the first five years of my recovery.

> THE TALLEST TREES ARE ALWAYS STRUCK BY
> LIGHTNING.
> —HERODOTUS

♪ *XVIII* ♪

Even Up on Misery Ave., They Sometimes Dance and Sing

*T*he complications caused by my brain injury were vast. And the confidence in my heart was one of the last qualities of my former self to consider returning. Regaining self-confidence was certainly the hardest thing to accomplish. If I needed a confidence boost, the only way I was going to get one was to make it happen. Sitting in the safe, silent obscurity of home was a comfort because I didn't want to be seen in such broken-down shape. But it wouldn't help me get back to living a life with any quality whatsoever.

My sister Shary says, "I remember Vince saying, 'Today I ran in my backyard!' He was trying to catch one of his dogs, Pup, from going over the fence, because he got tickets all the time for letting his dog run loose. Little Pup was getting arrested. Vince would cuss about having to go pay another ticket. And I remember him being really happy. He told me, 'I ran, I almost ran.'"

THE THINGS YOU'LL NEVER HAVE TO BE TAUGHT
   WILL BE THE HARDEST.
I'M SO NEAR, AND YET SO FAR. I DON'T KNOW WHAT
   TO DO.
WHERE MY HEART IS MY TREASURE IS.
PURSUE WITH PASSION.

I was straight-away into doing things that I was actually capable of in my physical condition. I got a greenhouse because I could grow things hydroponically. It didn't require strength or coordination, and it gave me a great return of fruits and vegetables. Not to mention the coveted herb. Every day I enjoyed the efforts along with the results. One of my challenges was to dig a 40-foot trench from the greenhouse to the little brown house for electricity. Big achievement. My balance was so bad that I couldn't lift one foot off the ground to push a shovel into the rocky soil. I had to hold on to the fence. But I dug that trench.

According to Bob, "Vince insisted that he be the one to dig the trench. It was hot, God dern, it was humid. Another friend of ours, Dale Voss, was there doing the wiring into the boxes, and I was on the back porch. Vince grabbed his shovel. He wasn't coordinated enough to even walk in a straight line, much less dig this trench—but he did it.

"I saw him not only sweating but with tears running down his face for most of the time. He'd stand up on the shovel with one foot and more than once just fall to the ground. But he'd get up and pick that shovel back up and start digging again. I tell you, it was a mark of determination that was a sign of things to come."

It seemed as if I hadn't seen anyone but doctors and therapists for the better part of a year, so I bought a ticket to Boston to visit Jim McGarry. Jim and I first met in 1970. I had just graduated from high school and hit the wandering road. Jim, Coley Baker, and I spent that summer to-gether in Oak Point, New York, on the St. Lawrence River.

"Vince had had his terrible accident, had risen from the dead, and was back on his feet, more or less." relates Jim McGarry. "He came to visit me in Cambridge, where I was living at the time. I guess he came to reconnect with a bit of his former life. That bit being me."

On my feet more or less, but I could barely walk with a cane. I sat in Jim's backyard of cherry trees and played games on his Apple IIE while waiting for him to return from his workday.

"One night," says Jim, "we headed out to find something to eat and came across a place in Harvard Square with a sign out front that said, 'Gutes Essen.' With a name like that we figured it was good for at least some decent beer and sausages with fried potatoes. In we went. By the second beer, the dinner came. I don't remember what we ordered, but on Vince's plate there was a big side order of red beets. I dug in to my dinner. Vince watched his beets.

"After a couple of minutes I asked, 'What's wrong, Vince? Don't like beets?'

"'I don't know.'

"I didn't respond. I didn't know if it might be scary not to know something so mundane about oneself."

"Then he said, 'Well, I guess I get to find out again.' Fork to beet, beet to mouth. Chew, swallow.

"'Well?' I asked.

"'I probably never liked beets.'

"'Sounds like you,' and I figured Vince would be OK."

Jim had just gotten into riding bicycles. I wanted to go along so badly. One of his routes was along the Charles River for several miles on either side. On the day we finally went, we struck out upriver on bicycle paths along the parkway headed inland. He was very patient with me. I could barely negotiate crawling up into the rider's seat.

Once I got to rolling, things settled down and I made some mileage just behind him. I was thrilled to be able to keep up. But riding along free like the breeze was a freedom that had its price. It wasn't long before we came to an intersection choked with commuter traffic. I found in short order that I did fine when I was pedaling along but when I had to stop at that intersection, I put the brakes on . . . and just fell over. I had no concept of what to do and no balance.

When I got up off the ground, though, I was a different person. I had ridden a bicycle again. I had felt the whistle of the wind. My poor elbows and knees were the worse for the wear, but I was smiling a smile of confidence that had not been there for a while. I was heartened beyond myself. The wordless fellow with the scorched shins and tears running down his cheeks reminded me of the old Vince. I took a punished but prouder self home to Providence Street.

EVEN UP ON MISERY AVE. THEY SOMETIMES DANCE
AND SING.

At one of my doctor visits that year, unimaginable surprises were waiting. It was with the arm that he rebuilt that I would teach myself one more time to fingerpick a completely new frailing on the guitar. He began our meeting by sitting across from me, with a clipboard and a pocket full of pens. I was on the bench, slowly twisting my right arm in the air in front of him.

He said, "Now, can you move the thumb for me?" With all my strength, I got it to twitch an almost unnoticeable amount. He jumped up from his chair and started to pace excitedly about the room, gasping, "I could not find those muscles in all that mush and blood. I didn't hook that up!" Examining closer, he said, "Keep it up, whatever you're doing. You'll get the use of it again."

Wow! I caned a little dazed from that doctor's office, thinking, *He didn't hook up what?* That even made the hair on the back of my neck, deadened to the touch, stand up for a split second.

I now started vocal and physical therapy three times a week. I went after my lessons with a vengeance to recoup the skills that would allow me to speak and walk normally again. I was one of their best pupils. I said more "firstly, lastly, costly, mostly, swiftly, ghastly, ghostlys" than anyone could imagine. My arm was in a whirlpool so long each week, it felt like I was going to mold. The extra work at home was on the trampoline. I counted between vocal exercises.

The following article appeared on the front page of the "Life/Style" section in the *Austin American-Statesman* on Thursday, August 18, 1983:

> "Song of Hope—Guitarist, Wife
> Fight Their Way Back from Accident"

> Vince Bell and wife, Melody, are the kind of accident victims who usually don't live to tell their story. In December, the Bells' car collided with another car being driven more than 60 miles per hour through a red light, according to police records. Vince was found unconscious 60 feet from his car with eye burns from lying in a pool of gasoline, head injuries and an almost-destroyed liver. While he lay in a coma for a month at Brackenridge Hospital, doctors discovered his left vocal cord was paralyzed and his right arm was fractured. Vince Bell had been a guitar player and singer for 13 years. A metal plate now holds together what's left of his arm bones.

> His wife suffered head and liver injuries, eye burns and 14 fractures. She's deaf in one ear and had surgery several times—"They're still digging the glass out of my body." Doctors are still determining the extent of their brain injuries. "It's like you have this warehouse full of knowledge, but because the brain is injured, it's extremely difficult to retrieve information," Melody said. "It's like constantly trying to unlock doors to your mind."

One day, Vince stood in the backyard crying, with his hands gripped around a shovel. "I tried to dig a hole and cried because I couldn't do it. There I was with a shovel and a brain and two arms, but I couldn't do it because I wasn't coordinated enough."

Those are the words of a man who used to be able to finger pick with his right hand while stretching the fingers on his left hand up and down and across the guitar's fret board. He could sing while he was doing all that. And he could make it look easy too, as the solo opener for performers like Dave Mason, David Crosby, and Delbert McClinton. Once he composed a rock ballet for former Houston Ballet choreographer James Clouser. His last gig was at Liberty Lunch, opening for Shawn Phillips.

"When I started therapy, I couldn't even talk," Vince said. "I couldn't remember anything. You really have to start from the very beginning again, going over very basic concepts. It was like getting drunk, but the morning after goes on for months."

Vince's daily challenge has been to master the basic routines most of us take for granted: how to make it around that corner, down the hall and into the bathroom; how to cook a meal, and not to forget to feed the poor cats. Everything he does is therapy. It took Vince a month to relearn the use of a lighter. He and Melody do exercises around the house to regain muscular control. Vince jumps on a trampoline and throws basketballs in the air. Melody does art work. They go to a physical therapist three times a week, and Vince goes to a vocal therapist. His left vocal cord has recently started to move after six months of therapy. Melody says doctors told them they would have been severely handicapped without intensive, frequent physical therapy. Melody seldom uses a cane to walk anymore.

When tragedy strikes, you find out who your friends are. In January, Stevie Ray Vaughan, Eric Johnson, Van Wilks and several other Austin musicians who are longtime pals of Vince, played a benefit to help him pay his medical bills.

"This is a totally justiceless event," said Vince, reigniting some of the anger that's cooled in the past months. "Somebody came along one night and this man nearly killed me and my wife and probably was fined $600 total. There's no justice for what has been taken away from me and my wife." There's no money to soften the blow, either. The other driver was cited for having no insurance and no driver's license. His blood alcohol level was measured at only .06, and he was not charged with DWI. "I had to make a decision—turn around and walk away and not hang on my resentment," Vince said. He started focusing on the things he could do something about. Anger softened into a determined acceptance and a will to survive.

"At first it was a physical tragedy. It changes from that to a more psychological problem. You start finding out you can learn again. Then it becomes: How well do you want to get? Are you happy talking this way? You deal with it. It's amazing what you can do when you set your mind to it.

"Now I need to sit down at a desk and write a song, then I can say, 'You're back in business, sonny boy.' I can rekindle the expertise. There's plenty of talent in there."

Life for the Bells is getting back to normal. Melody is happy she's able to drive now. Vince keeps looking at objects around his house that have been there for years as though he's seeing them for the first time. He has his eye on that guitar sitting in his music room.

He's also rediscovering Vince Bell the musician. "The only thing I could hold onto when I woke up from the coma was my work," Vince said. "I'd remember a song and I'd say, Old boy, you weren't a bad lyric poet. In 13 big ones, you may not remember much, but you must have done something right.

"Now it's just another hurdle. Just another event. I woke up and objectively realized that the party's not over. It will go on."

Vince Bell will be on the road again.

The interview smacked of my years of practice at it. Like most situations I would find myself in with other people, I tended to nervously talk faster, hoping it would take emphasis away from my real problems. The writer got some of it right as rain though. The part about therapy was so true. Without the work the therapists prescribed, I never could have disregarded so out-of-hand the observations of the doctors that I still had a partially paralyzed left vocal chord. No one still seemed to know whether I would walk again without the gaminess in my legs.

By September of 1983, though, I began to understand the depths to which I had been taken. The hurts in my body that had been so difficult to negotiate over the first nine months of my rehabilitation would seem like child's play when I brightened enough to realize what had happened to me. I was waging a helluva battle on all physical fronts, but I was losing the war now raging in my mind. I was angry about all I had lost. Emotionally, I was slowly losing my grasp. My life had been ended. My career was over a dozen years after it began in the coffeehouses of Houston.

FOREVER TAKES FOREVER.

I disappeared from all therapies. Again I put myself in a hospital, this time a mental institution north of Houston. I called my mother, saying, "You need to tie me to a tree somewhere because I'm losing the fight. I've put too much into getting better to have it all fall apart now. I think I need to see a doctor. I can't believe I'm saying this after this year, but help me find someone who can help."

♪ *XIX* ♪

Path of Least Regret

THE BEAST

To bring the beast back to life
you pull the stake from his heart.
He wakes up vicious and mean,
waits for the killing to start.
Like a bird of prey
in leather and steel,
he sets a vigil to stalk
those who would make him a meal.

He rides his metal and wheels
straight through the heart of the night.
Grinding his temper to hone
the sharpest blade he can find.
He cuts with merciless skill
the toughest feeling inside,
leaves it bare to the air
because there's no place to hide.

How many souls did you chain tonight,
to how many walls that hide the sky?
How many hopes were razed because of you?

Survivors number a few,
but seldom do come around.
They wear the scars on their face
from doing battle in town.
You might suspect they would steal
to someplace where it's safe,
Instead they go see the beast
to throw some scrap in the cage.

The psychiatric hospital north of Houston was solemn as death during my first few days there. I never realized just how self-conscious I was about seeing anyone in the mindless condition I floundered in. Because I had acknowledged to myself that I was losing the struggle, I lost some hard-fought, frightfully-won ground. I checked in on my 32nd birthday. My dogs, Buffy and Pup, and the cats would just have to do without me for a time.

Report of psychological evaluation:

Past medical history: Patient spent approximately two months in a hospital in Austin, and he had more than one operation for his liver problem and has been having physical therapy and speech therapy. He regained consciousness and slowly he had been regaining his memory and some of his ability to play a guitar; however, he had not been able to work ever since the accident. The patient became increasingly depressed after the accident. He has been very depressed, having crying spells. The patient has been seen by different doctors since his accident and he has been taken off and on medications for depression, but none has helped.

The patient at the time of the evaluation was oriented to person, time, and place. The patient's sensorium was clear, affect at times blunted, mood depressed, insight and judgment were age-appropriate. The patient denied all types of hallucinations and delusions. He did report suicidal ideation but no tendencies. The patient also reported a history of substance use to primarily marijuana and beer. The patient's speech was very low in terms of volume, output was extremely high, as a matter of fact the patient talked almost incessantly throughout the evaluation. His thinking process appeared to be quite rigid but free of loose associations, tangential thinking or florid thoughts. The patient worked on all the tasks assigned, and the data collected is an accurate representation of his psychological state.

"Visiting hours were at night, and Mother and I and some of the other family members would go to see Vince," Shary says. "His mood swings continued, and he would go from laughing one minute to crying the next, to extreme violence the next. We were really afraid he was going to hurt himself.

"It wasn't like hospitals today where it's very interactive and everybody gets the family in on things and into group. Vince would go to group but none of the family was involved. He kept his spirits up as well as he could, but he'd say, 'I just can't help it, I can't control myself.' He was very depressed about that."

Unfortunately, it remained beyond me to recall the people who came to visit. I wouldn't remember that any of my family came to see me.

I spoke to no one for my first three days there, sitting in a chair by the window in a commons area. On the window was a tree frog. It seemed like he had been there for days. Perhaps we both had been. Tiny, bright shades of green he was with large, interested red eyes. It didn't seem like there was anything or anyone else in the place but happy, busy little him. And me. I thought if he could talk, maybe we both could.

"Wanna cup of coffee?" he said.

"Sure." Surprised, I turned in my seat to see a strong-looking man in his fifties with a short, military haircut. He walked into the automated blue Masonite kitchen alcove, grabbed a cup from the counter, and handed it to me. I astonished myself by saying, "Thanks." Rubbing my forehead, "How long have I been here"?

"Several days I know of," he replied.

I thought, *What a good fellow.*

"Who are you?"

"I'm John from Waller. I'll be your roommate down the hall. You must be Vince," he said, obviously trying to pull the answer out of me easily.

"How'd you know?"

He gestured with one finger, "The name tag."

I fumbled at my three-day-old T-shirt and felt the adhesive-backed paper stuck to it.

"So why don't we sit together at lunch today?" John asked me. The thick ice finally broke at the mental institution in the Woodlands nine months after I had been laid down on the freeway feeder road in that Central Texas college town.

When I turned back to the window, the tree frog was gone. I wished him well.

In the afternoons I would meet the therapists, the floor nurses, and the nice lady at the pill window. These people were your lifeline friends in a place where the institution locked the doors after you voluntarily admitted yourself. I would find it much harder to get out of this building than it was to get in, even though it had cost a small fortune to enter.

We patients played it very close to the chest. We never talked about our conditions or medications. In the evening, we would line up at the pill window to receive our prescriptions in little white envelopes. Like desperate players in a card game, no one would allow any of the others to see what hand they were playing. Some, like me, would only get a couple of lightweight sleeping pills. Others needed some pretty heavyweight drugs just to remain civil and controllable. On a couple of occasions, we would see one another screamingly, ravingly out of control, mostly in the middle of the night. Sometimes we would turn over in our beds in the morning and one of us would be gone. Sometimes we would be released by our physicians. You had to care about anyone leaving that place, because you could not ignore the hurt and disillusionment you could see behind a good person's eyes. They were all good.

I had one new visitor once or twice a week. She was a very distant connection to my former world, but for some reason I didn't want to see anyone else. She came to see me a half-dozen times. I would only remember one. Her name was Sarah.

Sarah described her visits with me as far-flung, fragmented talks with no beginning, middle, or end to the conversation. "We used to sit in a long hall with plants and couches against one wall, and glass on another," Sarah says. "You were so small then, very thin. I would call you in the afternoon so that you would know that I was coming. But when I got there, you wouldn't remember that I had called. You would ask, 'What are you doing here?'

"We would sit in that hallway, or the cafeteria, and you would talk endlessly of what you were thinking about. It was impossible to follow. I didn't know the references, and it was impossible to make sense of. It was like being dropped into the middle of somebody else's stream of consciousness, their life, with no lead-up, no segues, no explanations. There was a sense of terrible urgency. You were an overwhelming outpouring. It wasn't conversing. You were consumed by whatever it was at the moment—lyrics to your songs, for instance. It's just a guess, but I don't think you really had any sense of time—past, present, or future. It was all there together at the same time, memories and things you wanted to do tomorrow and what you were doing right then."

Behavioral observations:

The purpose of the evaluation was to assist in determining how much of the patient's present behavior is an artifact of the closed head injury. He smiled frequently, spoke continually throughout the evaluation. There were also a lot of metaphors and colorful analogies that the patient used, but he seemed to rapidly lose track of what he was talking about and stated that this was something new as a result of the head injury. Since the automobile accident which occurred in December of 1982, the patient has experienced significant decrease in his overall brain functioning. There are indications of short-term memory deficits and clear motor-coordination problems. At the time of coming out of the coma, the patient states that he could not walk, talk, go to the bathroom, balance himself, or play the guitar but felt like some of these things were coming back. His ability to use his right arm, which is his dominant arm, was significantly below expectancy. Further, the patient's ability to walk was impaired as a result of closed-head injury. His short-term memory seemed to be sporadic at best.

Psychological techniques:

Rorschach Inkblot Technique

Response to card #1: "A young fellow playing a violin. He will cradle his violin and learn to read and write music. My future for this young man is that he will learn the score and someday write his own."

Response to card #7: "I see a father gazing at his son. I see the son with problems. A prior picture would show the son in a lot of trouble."

Response to card #11: "I seem to see individuals herding cattle over a bridge. They are monitored by a dragon. He is out looking for a morsel of food. In the future I can see these individuals herding these cattle up the hill. It is not a climb as much as it is a struggle. It is an uphill struggle. The road ahead is not clear. I anticipate a successful crossing."

Finally to card #15 the patient started to really fragment as he stated: "Ah, in the photo I see no one mourning a death. I see a person that is the devil. I see a lot of death before me. There is a raft of tombstones. This individual is some keeper. He is what you would call a gatekeeper. He is not mourning, he is surveying. He looks well suited for the job. Before this photo I see a hill with briars, small trees, pastoral view and an absence of activity aside from bees and other insects. Sunlight is not obvious. In the future I see stones falling with people's names in the dirt. I don't mean that badly. I see no graveyard at all. Trees are making their way through and tombstones are on their stumps. I don't see the individual there. Maybe his is one of the stones. A graveyard is in despair. Overgrowth everywhere. This cycle returned the natural odd sense of normalcy. There is justice to this scenario."

It's important to point out again that the bulk of this seems to be directly related to the accident, the significant change in lifestyle, the movement from being a relatively independent free spirit to a very dependent and almost helpless individual. This has been a great deal more than this patient simply has been able to accommodate.

The number of responses that the patient gave would suggest that his level of cognitive functioning is probably in the above-average range. Most of his responses were F plus, although there were several F minuses noted. Primary determinate used was color as well as form.

There was no indication of any type of thought disorder noted; however, there were clear indications of just positively unrequited anger, frustration and also a higher than normal expectancy with regard to fire content.

Passive individuals such as the patient of this type show a curious detachment from their own antisocial behavior and its consequences. They appear to feel themselves as victimized by their impulses as are those who suffer directly from them, and their attitudes imply the underlying notion that it is not I who am doing this, the impulses and the results are beyond my control. The patient also seems to be using a lot of fantasy as a means of putting limits to the experience and uses this fantasy as a receptor for the inveterate anger that he has built up.

Summary and conclusion: The depression that the patient is experiencing does not appear to be organic in nature, rather the depression seems to be an artifact of the inability to accept the terrible ordeal that he has undergone. Consequently, he is left with trying to make some sense out of something that in essence has no sense. The anger that is a result of this terrible perpetration to him has prompted the depression.

An artist-in-residence showed me how to make a leather belt and a clay ashtray. I thought she understood me the best. She also helped me convince the administrative higher-ups that I should be let off the wing every day to run a mile or so around the building.

I slowly, jerkily limped around that hospital convinced that I would again run like the wind. Someday. By the time I left the place, I was far off yesterday's pace but I needed track shoes. An admiring hall mate of mine named Sandy came up to me in the commissary one day after the run. "Is it getting any easier?" No doubt she referred to my halting and uneven gait.

"No, but that's OK. It will."

"You have such confidence. Did your doctor prescribe the exercise?"

"No, but that's OK, too."

"Listen, Vince, I got something for your birthday. See if this fits." She opened a little case containing a finely made, burnished silver and gold wristwatch.

I put that wristwatch on that day and seldom removed it. Like the rain gauge at home, I would just stare at it admiringly. It became my little confidant that would quietly, calmly, beautifully tick away the unending moments of my repair into the years to come.

My attending physician and I didn't get along because he thought I was confused and didn't make sense.

Oh surely (i.e., no shit).

I still could barely keep my head on straight or write my name on a check, much less talk well. So I didn't give a rat's ass what the man thought. His criticisms of me were counterproductive when I so needed someone, anyone, in the huge medical machine I turned to for help to tell me, "You'll be all right. Just work as hard as you can imagine, for as long as you can stand, and then get up and work some more. But you'll be all right." He never gave me the time of day more often than he was required. I was paying one thousand insurance dollars a day to keep him preening, but I probably saw him for 30 minutes in a week. I was damned if I was going to be trod on by a spectator on the way to his golf cart.

One of my most important efforts during my time there didn't have anything to do with my ever-tumbling relations with the professionals. It was directed toward remembering the lyrics I had written over the first decade of my career.

Some of those poetries had come from my first travels out of high school in upstate New York on the St. Lawrence River at the Thousand Islands on that BMW R60. Others were from Princeton, Pennsylvania Dutch country, the Wisconsin Dells, the Colorado Rockies and Raton, New Mexico, Reno, the Carson Valley plain, and the Sierra around Truckee and Lake Tahoe. The big towns like New York City, San Francisco, Los Angeles, Houston, and Washington had their references too. Jigsawing my memories together read to me like a fragmented but understandable trip itinerary. It told me who I was. Where I had been. When and with whom. I cherished those recollections. Whether anyone else thought I was playing with a full deck or no, I had found a window back into the past. I could start building again from this new foundation.

I bought a blue spiral notebook at the hospital store and flew into reminiscing with those left-behind slivers of song. It made me very proud to hear that hardworking young writer grappling with such complex language. My heart breathed that day one of the few breaths of the year that felt like someone had lifted a weight from me. I was a forever away from any kind of comprehensive knowledge of my former self, but the person I was finding in the lyrics was very ambitious. I could respect that.

For the first time in nine wayward months, it was interesting and edifying to remember yesterday. I no longer feared what I couldn't revive. I was inspired to work ever harder to regain the misplaced. That which was taken from me I could find, if only I would be brave enough and trudge onward.

Many songs were long gone, though, left smeared on that stretch of highway more than 150 miles to the west. Of others I could only recall a line or two. Over my time in the hospital, I ultimately pieced together parts of some 30 songs, enough to inspire me to complete the entire catalogue eventually. At first, it was a fright to recognize how little I could remember. But I stuck with it day after day. One song would hint of another. It was quite a research. Word by word, phrase by phrase, the songs I wrote in the '70s returned like flocking birds. Only a precious wandering few at first, followed by others until I was surrounded by the perky little dears.

Discharge Summary
Patient name: Vince Bell
Admitting diagnosis: Major depressive disorder, single
episode
Discharge diagnosis: Post-traumatic injury

This is a thin, white male who was very tremulous in his speaking. He is very vague and tends to wander at times. On several occasions he is tearful, and his judgment seems to be poor. He seemed to be passive in many ways, and at times would show sudden outbursts of anger for which he would later apologize profusely. After some time he began to respond to treatment, and his mood improved markedly. However, his contact in therapy continued to be superficial even to the time of discharge. He did not seem to be totally committed to a process of psychotherapy.

TIME WILL WORK FOR ME.

When I arrived back in Austin six weeks later, at Providence Street everything looked normal, deceptively the same. Nothing major appeared changed, especially the unplanned neighborhood with long grass between the disarray of cluttered little houses. The front door opened easily onto a setting I remembered. A small but comfortable sleeper sofa, a dinner table, unmatched chairs, and a sideboard. The nicest garage-sale furniture. My furniture. Grimy ceiling fans slowly turned above the scene. The place could obviously use some attention. My dogs' toenails clicked on the scarred, worn hardwood floors as they squealed and jumped up on me. The cats circled curious figure-eights between my legs to see if I had anything for them to eat. I could tell they were glad to see me. I was so glad to see them.

In the back room, the keys were yellowing and dusty on the little 63-key parlor piano. It was next to the tacky French desk that looked out the window. The typewriter was just as I had left it. The guitar was propped up in the corner by a festively colored calendar from a favorite Mexican restaurant. Its strings were crusted and green. It was like seeing a now rough-looking old friend you had everything in common with once upon a time. Someone you never dreamed could drift so far away.

Many typewritten snippets of poetry were haphazardly tacked to the walls. My grandmother's canned goods were stacked on shelves in the kitchen. When I opened the back door, the tiny back-porch steps were still rotting away next to the wooden water-heater housing. In the middle of the large, unmown backyard was the hydroponic greenhouse, big as a two-car garage.

Everything seemed in its place but . . . my wife was gone. Her drawers and wardrobes were empty. Her suitcases were missing. I felt badly for her. I felt badly for myself. Neither she nor I, after that collision of Christmas week, were in shape to continue as we had. We had both became brain injured that night. The only difference in the severity of our conditions was that she had required shorter hospitalization. As the months progressed, we had grown further apart. The journey for us both became solitary, desolate, abandoned, forsaken. For head injury victims, there are no two alike. That helped to keep us speeding in different directions. Our inevitable divorce was just a formality. My temper had always been hair-trigger. Now it was worse. Frustrations grew out of control as neither of us could even mount an orgasm because of the scrambled synapses in our spinal cords. We certainly couldn't help one another.

Hell, we couldn't help ourselves. The relationship we had enjoyed for several years was doomed by the backwash of one Christmas-week night.

That first day back home, I sat silently swaying on the front porch swing, thinking about the cuckoo's nest of a hospital. It was a comfort to see life going on just like before on either side of the little brown house on Providence Street. Ira still worked and Mary still gardened. The neighborhood wasn't missing a beat. From here on out, I thought to myself, neither would I.

♪ *XX* ♪

Music School

1-1-84: POT OF COFFEE. NEW TYPEWRITER. YO, MUST
   BE A NEW YEAR.
GOOD MORNING, BLACKIE, GOOD MORNING.

*F*or years I had kept that series of Black Books. Every writer must have one, I believed. Each consisted of 300 pages filled with musings in my own hand. Now that I could write again, I used the black books to goad myself into believing that I could do what I must to return some quality to life. I needed them to determine if it was possible to accomplish the most frustrating goals. And the goals were simple. It was just that I was unable to do anything I did before. From a place where nothing was familiar, I would write down quotes from famous people and passages from other artists. There were observations on authorship. Notes to myself about the works I could write, the works I should write, were all there. They were my counterpart, my calculator, my advisor, and my pal when I was lonely.

> I'VE GOT TO JUSTIFY THE HOUR BY COMING IN
> HERE EACH AND EVERY HOUR AND WRITING
> SOMETHING DOWN.
> LEARN HOW TO WRITE AGAIN.
> THERE'S INSPIRATION EVERY DAY, YOU JUST
> STUMBLED ON IT BEFORE.
> I MUST WHIP THIS "SUDDEN DEATH" LIKE A
> STEPCHILD.

It wasn't so much a diary, this old Black Book, but a writer's collection of thoughts. In the glimmer of a lone comment it provided the simple perspective, sometimes predictable, sometimes outrageous, but always of value. Like a sculptor with a chisel in his hand, wearily staring down a block of stone, I was given an unscarred surface to mold. I refined my thoughts to a razor's edge of believability in the pages of those notebooks.

"I'VE SEEN THIS BEFORE, YOU'RE HOLING UP UNTIL YOU GET IT RIGHT," said a quote from my pal Stephen Jarrard. Sometimes I would write down a line or two about a subject and leave it to a later intuition. I would attempt to write at least one line of the truth. That was harder than you might suppose. The odd outlooks, or the novel viewpoints, or just plain weird parts of speech used in unconventional ways were the seeming point to this. Since the wreck, there was no shortage of odd perspectives.

> SOMEONE IS CRYING FOR HELP. IT'S TIME YOU WIPE
> YOUR NOSE AND LISTEN TO ANOTHER SONG.
> THERE IS A POSITION OPEN AT THE TOP OF THE
> FOOD CHAIN.
> AN EVENT LIKE THIS WILL MAKE YOU SCRAMBLE
> FOR THE LIFEBOATS. AND THERE AREN'T ENOUGH
> LIFEBOATS.
> CAN YOU WRITE? SLOW DOWN AND WRITE.

PEACE IS NOT THE ABSENCE OF CONFLICT. IT IS THE
    ABILITY TO COPE WITH IT.
IT'S NOT HOW YOU ACCOMPLISH VICTORY, IT'S HOW
    YOU ACCEPT DEFEAT.

I had been entering thoughts faithfully into those now fraying
tomes for years. Like a security blanket, that assembly of my best current thinking had gone everywhere my guitar had. It was the place I
could go to tell my thoughts when the loneliness of the '70s music
circuits overwhelmed me. In those pages, no one could disagree or
think less of me for considering the reasoning I put up. That simple
organization had given me song after song since I began to write as
a 19-year-old kid. The Black Book routine was another part of my
identity that I unwillingly left behind.

Not until the new year of 1984 did I force that habit again. I began
to fill a new book up with whatever scatterings I could muster, sometimes hour by hour when in the middle of some challenging theme.

RISING FROM THE ASHES? CRAWLING FROM THE
    WRECKAGE.
IT MAY BE NOTHING. CREATE SOMETHING FROM
    NOTHING. WRITE IT DOWN.
ON THE OTHER SIDE OF THE GRAVE THE MUSIC'S
    STILL GOOD.
MY HANDS ARE WAKING UP.

"Nobody thought Vince would ever play again," my acoustic col-
league Steven Fromholz says. "Nobody except Vince."

In the back room at Providence Street, that crusty old Martin that
had fingerpicked me from Idaho to Mexico on the National Coffeehouse Circuit sat silently in its case. The bronze strings were shades
of cloying green, and they flaked like molting snakeskin from oxida-
tion. The ebony fret board was stained by a deteriorating chemistry.

That left faint, reminiscently vermilion lines across the frets down the neck of the instrument. That piece of wood and steel that had lost me as a partner was sitting forgotten, under forgotten past-performance posters, looking like broken-down me. It was always watching, never moving or making a sound. That expressionless, forlorn-looking guitar would face me, stony and silent, with the sweat stains from a previous decade of play dates iced across that now cracked and aging varnished spruce.

Perhaps now I was taking some precious steps toward being able to do something with the love of music again. Though I had not noticed my six-string very much in the last year, that was subtly, imperceptibly changing. However, since my right arm was so weak, I found that my old buddy, the dark-top acoustic, was too difficult to play. The strings over the fret board were just non-negotiable for the nerve-damaged kid.

During this dimmest of times I heard one of the few knocks on the front door of Music School, my little shiplap frame house. Music School was an invention of mine to inspire my enthusiasm for the unbelievable amount of retooling I would have to do to ever see the wings of a stage again.

Rap, rap, rap.

"Yeah . . . just a minute," I said, shaking off a grogginess I wore like a cheap suit for most of the '80s. When I opened the door there stood, like a vision, Townes Van Zandt, without the silver tooth. It had been many moons since that frigid primer on the patio in Houston, and we two had shut down as many bars with our tunes as most other players had played since then. But we led our constantly twisting and turning musical lives like night trains, so we had rarely seen each other at the clubs.

Before I could get a word in edgewise, he put a hand on my shoulder and uneasily blurted, "I named a kid after you and Wrecks Bell."

He pulled a square little black and white photo from his top pocket that showed him holding tiny William Vincent Van Zandt.

He sat for a moment and tried to make some sense of busted up me, "Where can I put this for you so you might find it again?" Waving the photo.

"Leave it in the bowl with the keys. Everything I am aware of these days is there." In a heartbeat, though, my kindly pal was gone.

Oh well. Figuring I better move along if I thought I ever had a chance to find my way back, I asked my sister Shary to loan me one of her J. D. Rich six-strings that played more easily, and I put extra-light strings on it. I started trying to be a piano player for the first time, as well. Every day the stoic dark-top sat in the stand beside my writing desk, like a long-ago desire unfulfilled. It saw every unending rehearsal on the parlor piano and at the strange new guitar. I used to think of it as waiting for me till I was stronger. And stronger I was gonna get. Come hell or high water.

> MUSIC IS NOT A UNIVERSAL LANGUAGE, IT'S A
>   PERSONAL CODE.
> IT'S 5 O'CLOCK IN THE MORNING, THE LIGHT'S ON
>   AT MUSIC SCHOOL.
> THROUGH SIMPLISTIC EXERCISES I'M RECALLING
>   TIME, BEAT, FEEL, TOUCH, RELAXATION.

"He called his thing 'Music School,'" Bill Browder says. "He was going back and trying to play guitar, and talking about having to relearn his own songs. It seems like it was at least two years before he could really play at all. His voice was still hoarse, barely above a whisper."

The music of the songs I had authored before the wreck was lost to me. "Did I write this music?" I had to hear the songs on tape to know they were my own. I would then distantly remark, "That's a good tune." My sadness was great about not being able to recognize my own previous works.

On the wall beside the desk was a stack a foot and a half high of cassette tapes of the former Vince Bell's various musical incarnations. They included Vince Bell bands and Vince Bell solos, duets, and trios. The earliest tapes were of me playing other people's songs. The later ones had only my own compositions. The venues they represented were from concerts, clubs, coffeehouses, colleges, radio stations, and TV shows. From them I began to reintroduce myself to a musical yesterday still far beyond my grasp.

"Music School was designed specifically to rehabilitate himself back into his world and remember who Vince Bell was," according to Bob Sturtevant. "He had to remember his songs and remember what it was he did on the guitar, though he couldn't do it on the guitar anymore. I'd sit with him, and he'd go through the songwriting process."

I was determined to sing again. I didn't care about doctors' reports or vocal cords. Singing was in the heart. I was surprised to find how few people seemed to know that. Sing with a paralyzed vocal cord? How will I play a musical instrument when I can't keep a beat? Better yet, how will I re-teach myself to play not one, but two major instruments: guitar and piano?

By 1984, my overwhelming difficulties with every physical and mental capability brought the sobering realization that I might never again be that rock 'n' western songwriter dude from the '70s. I wasn't even a good handicap at this point. All the driving from one town to the next, and all the song-playing night to night, was done. Poor old drooling, stuttering Vince had been seriously foreshortened. I was making bantam but essential progress in all aspects of music, though, by laboring at that parlor piano, not yet with the familiar old guitar.

Bob Sturtevant again: "Vince tried to play but it was very difficult for him. Mainly he would just chord with his left hand. He didn't have any coordination with his right hand. That would get frustrating, so he'd go over and play on the piano. He couldn't play the piano worth a flip, either."

I rehearsed my music unfailingly. I did physical and vocal work unfailingly. I wrote in the Black Book unfailingly, and I traveled to see my family and my friends Stephen and Franci.

And that was all I did.

> JUST GET STRENUOUS, DON'T GET CREATIVE, JUST
>   STRENUOUS.
> THE HUNCHBACK OF MUSIC SCHOOL.
> A CHAISE LOUNGE, A TYPEWRITER, AND A GUITAR.

Stephen and Franci Files Jarrard were dear friends during these days. I would visit them at their home in Elgin, outside Austin, and they made my isolation more livable by building some glass shelves over the windows on the sun side of the back room that had become my music rehearsal room. After the shelves were done, they left me with some ivy plants to set on the shelves, which helped create a pleasant atmosphere where I was proud to work.

"We were there and supportive," Stephen says. "At first we just visited and later, when he could, we played music. What I remember about Vince then was that he moved slowly, and the way he talked—it was laborious but he did it. He just worked at it, and he trained. He was like a boxer.

"He called his house a 'Music School' because he was teaching himself—working his hands up to playing guitar again. He was teaching his fingers, arms, and hands to do it. I was able to show him how to exercise his fingers for strength training. I was very admiring of his stamina and courage to do all of that."

I dreamed of performing again, but I could play precious few notes on the guitar. I could see a G chord on the fret board in my mind, but my left hand no longer knew how to finger a G chord. After spending a young lifetime at the discipline of music like all my other pals, it looked sickeningly like they would go onward without me. I started seriously considering that I might never see my associates again. The wager was my pitiful life. I kept telling myself it was worth it.

"Words and feelings rather than structured songwriting came to him first," Kathleen recalls. "He started to have a flood of feelings and emotions, things he wanted to write down, wanted somehow to let out. Like Mozart who heard everything in his head, Vince could hear all the music in his head, and all the words and emotions were there, but the outlet for it was gone.

"Even writing things down was still a difficult process for him. It was all flying through his head, but communicating it was the trick now. That had always been his life—being the master communicator. His calling card had been that he could write it down better, or differently, and move another human being with it. That the communication piece was missing was very frustrating for him. He would talk nonstop to the point of exasperation and exhaustion. Then there would be depression that would come from that, over and over again."

> IT IS EVER THE MORE DIFFICULT TO MAKE THESE
>   AWKWARD MUSICAL MOVES LOOK EASY. I WILL
>   NOT REST UNTIL I AM THE BEST.
> MORE VOCAL PUSH-UPS.
> AH. UP INTO THE JET STREAM OF MUSIC AT 100 BEATS
>   PER MINUTE.
> DON'T LET THE DISSATISFACTION OF A MOMENT
>   DISSUADE YOU.

Bob remembers, "The months went by, and it was a matter of months, not days or weeks, he was that persistent. I really think it was his insistence on learning how to get a beat back that aided in his recovery in a variety of ways. It was a form of therapy, not only physical but mental therapy. Had he not been so driven in his music, he might not have come back as fast, or maybe not as much. His life was rehab, and everything he did was rehab. I've never met a more hardheaded man. He was absolutely determined, and this permeated everything."

> MUSIC IS STILL BIGGER THAN LIFE.
> I'M NOT THIS WAY BECAUSE I'M A MUSICIAN, I'M A MUSICIAN BECAUSE I'M THIS WAY.
> MUSIC IS MY MISTRESS.
> BREATHING EXERCISES, MICROSETS, COUNTING, ARPEGGIOS, ATONAL SCALES.
> TODAY'S REHEARSAL SAYS YOU'RE GETTING MORE BEAT-ORIENTED.

What was most bedeviling was that I could not keep a consistent beat with either foot or with my hands. As they say in music, I couldn't count to four anymore, at least not with any regularity. That had to happen before much of the music rehabilitation could even begin. As a result, I began working toward making music on the little 63-key parlor piano, something that would involve both my hands and feet. I would teach my hands and my feet rhythms and chord forms over and over until the routine turned into a long-term memory that my mind could grasp. It would take all of that year and into the next to just relearn the basics of keeping a simple beat and forming chords on either of the two instruments.

I worked into a four-track tape machine through a parametric EQ that was permanently set up in Music School on a rolling TV tray. It could be moved about the space. I set up a microphone for vocals and piano. A direct input for the guitar ran into an amplifier. I couldn't play a piece consistently or well, but I could do my best into the recording equipment and corner an acceptable rendition of the new songs sooner or later.

> I HAD TO CAPO UP FOR THE FIRST TIME!
> I THINK I CORNERED A SONG.
> HELP HIM TO WRITE BETTER.

I've never liked to start pieces that I couldn't finish, but some songs sat around for a long time until I was writer enough to approach the theme. It was the classic duel between the seeker with an idea and the story that dares to be told. Every new work was a challenge to my "write nothing twice" ideal of authorship.

In the master-slave of it all, the tune is the master and the author is the slave until the piece is written. The struggle in between is a no-holds-barred free-for-all. Seeker seeking, elusive artwork bobbing and weaving. Sometimes the seekers don't even get close. You build them to perform, these songstuffs. You imbue them with all the strengths of a good composition, then put them aside with all the others of different nature and kind. Then let something else complicate your life.

The characteristic distinction I allowed each one from another in beat, meter, rhyme scheme, subject matter, and style made the tall ones tall, the short ones short. The fat ones were truly fat, and the skinny ones, skinny as hell. Every new work taught this intrepid creator something or other about authorship that he probably hadn't known before. It's one of the reasons a writer writes. Learning about oneself and the rest of the world in this manner is so honest, so private. Like absorbing any good morsel of work, the revelations are more apt to be indelible. The technique behind learning from a piece provides all the incentive a gutsy explorer craves.

Listening to the cassette tapes of my old self scared me into realizing that I could have been discovered and discarded by some monolithic, multinational record label before I had learned some of the musical lessons that were to come. The writer and musician I was slowly metamorphosing into was much more than the talented kid I had been in those earlier recordings.

> HERE'S TO THE STUDENT AND THE TEACHER, VINCE.
> THE UNINFORMED TEACHING THE UNIMPRESSED.
> BAD AS IT IS, IT COULDN'T BE GOING BETTER THAN
>   THIS.
> DAMAGED BOY REINVENTS MUSIC.

"At this time I was kind of going to Music School, too," Bob Sturtevant says. "Vince began exploring all the basics of what it took to write a song. Watching his process, and the way his songs evolved, helped me to understand the nature of songwriting. He just steadily improved, steadily, steadily. It was blood, sweat, and tears every step of the way. It occurred to me that maybe it was blood, sweat, and tears every step of the way whether you are head-injured, or not.

"I knew he was going to make it if he could just keep his level of determination. His personal life continued to take a toll on him, but in the midst of it he never relinquished Music School. That seemed to be the anchor, his primary anchor."

"I saw him play in his house some," observes Mandy Mercier. "I remember thinking that could be a lifeline. You can't figure out what makes you play music anyway—it's a different part of your brain. That could bring him back. If he could play the guitar—like a sense memory—if he could do that, it would give him a tree to hang the other stuff on."

In the first couple of months of 1984, I was able to sing and play "I Shall Be Released," by Bob Dylan, on the guitar Shary had given me. That was the first song for me since Christmas week of 1982. "Pair of

Dice" was the first piece of music I would write, 15 months after my wreck. It was simple lyrically, clever, and yet more sophisticated musically than I was able to perform at that time. Its music was a nameless but finished piece from before the wreck that had required relearning. Its lyric was my first attempt at rhyming the King's English again. It was an arrangement that I completed and played on the piano initially. "Pair of Dice" and several other early songs from 1984 would be somewhat playable on both instruments in the privacy of my home. It all showed me that my idea of a Music School was working.

PAIR OF DICE

A luckless night,
after a luckless day.
The frying fish commits filet.
The waitress was a plate of babe.
He eyed the price.
A pair of dice.

Before the morning
light she glides
back and forth
and through the night.
She thinks of him
between the bites.
A pair of dice.

I'm wild as the streets,
high as the sky,
free for forever,
and yours if you'd like.
See me, stop me, tell me goodnight.
But, you don't
even know me,
do you?

Back up on the boulevard.
There's a very few of us,
there's a very lot of them.
They're like hawks and sparrows,
spiders and flies,
and a pair of dice . . .
like you and I.

I was just out of my high school football helmet when this practice promo photo was taken in 1970.

From author's collection, photographer unknown.

My first promotional poster done in 1971. The background is the swamp behind Addicks Dam off Texas State Highway 6, outside Houston.

From author's collection, photographer unknown.

When I started gigging I would play for anyone who would book me. I was on a mission even on this Sunday dawn show, right after the Farm Report, on KHOU-TV in Houston.

From author's collection, photographer unknown.

If any photo can be a portrait of my early years in music, this is it, at the Old Quarter in Houston.

From author's collection, photographer unknown.

Playing lunch at Anderson Fair with Sandy Mares. We got paid in spaghetti and beer.

From author's collection, photographer unknown.

A sunny afternoon on the patio at Anderson Fair. "We called the shots, we made the rules, spaghetti bars were our music schools" I wrote in my song, "The Fair."

Photo by Jerry Walsh.

A '70s calendar at the Fair during a time when we might not have known which day of the week it was, but we knew, month by month, who was on this calendar.

Austin era promo for Moon Hill Management by Dick Reeves Design.

From author's collection, photographer unknown.

The poster for the ballet named after one of my songs, "Bermuda Triangle."

Soaking up a couple of DosXX in the cabin on Snake Street in Kings Beach, CA, on the north shore of Lake Tahoe.

From author's collection, photographer unknown.

I took this photo of Music School with a 35mm Pentax I got from the Texas Rehabilitation Commission in about 1983 or 1984. Never found anything better to relate the queerness of the period.

This was taken by James Minor, my photography professor at Austin Community College.

Hobart Taylor, Greg Freeman and I while recording the songs for the *Complete Works* at Low Down Studios under the Bay Bridge.

Photo by Frank Martin.

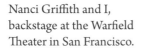Nanci Griffith and I, backstage at the Warfield Theater in San Francisco.

Photo by Steve Jennings.
Courtesy of Hobart Taylor.

Recording *Phoenix* at Hyde Street Studio in the "Tenderloin District" of San Francisco.

Photo by Tom Erikson.

Recording *Phoenix* with (back row) Fritz Richmond, Geoff Muldaur, (front row) Bob Neuwirth and me.

Photo by Frank Martin.

Phoenix cover art when it was a work-in-progress. The photo, by Wyatt McSpadden, was taken in a Texas grain silo.

At the Paradiso in Amsterdam. "This stage swallows singer/songwriters, but not Vince."
—Bert Van De Camp, *Oor Magazine*.

Photo by Sarah Wrightson.

Iain Mathews, Eric Taylor, and I trade tunes in Zurich, Switzerland.

Photo by Sarah Wrightson.

Mark Olsen, of The Jayhawks, and I backstage at Pop in de Poort, Groningen, Netherlands.

Photo by Sarah Wrightson.

Onstage at the Bottom
Line in New York City,
June 1995.

*Photo by Renee
Bouth-Tsanjoures.*

The last time I saw Van Zandt was at the Cactus Cafe in Austin.

Photo by Sarah Wrightson.

Backstage in 2000 at the Bottom Line in New York: Lyle Lovett, Steven Fromholz, myself, Guy Clark, and Willis Alan Ramsey with Alan Pepper in the fore.

From author's collection, photographer unknown.

Lyle, Victor Krauss, and I rehearsing my songs that we will do together on *Austin City Limits*, 2000.

Photo by David Roth.

With Lyle and the band performing in front of the ACL studio audience the next day.

Photo by David Roth.

Mainstage at the Kerrville Folk Festival, 2005.

Photo by Brian Kanof.

♪ **XXI** ♪

Edge of the World

"**I** don't know the physiology of traumatic brain injury," Stephen Jarrard says, "but the difficulty seemed to be not that Vince was not the same person but that he couldn't remember who he had been, what he liked or didn't like, wanted or didn't want. If he'd done something, or thought something, or felt something, he didn't remember it. In other words, he was himself, but he didn't remember himself."

Bob Sturtevant says, "Vince talked for a long time like there were two of him. He would refer to himself as 'we.' 'This is what "we're" doing today.' There was Vince, and there was Vince the watcher. I'd ask him, 'What have you been doing today?' He'd say, 'Well, we've been working in Music School.'"

The early part of 1984 found me feeling battle-fatigued and solemn. Memories were filtering in piecemeal, while it remained beyond me in large part to master my emotions. Lost abilities to taste, walk, talk, balance, and recall, coupled with the pain in my arm, taunted me. But the animals were there with plenty of love to go around between old Buff, the Australian heeler, Pup, the tiny poodle mix, the cats, and me.

We'd all stand around the gas space-heaters that winter, wiggling until we were warm. Music School, where dogs and cats usually flew about, was now dark and cold. And quiet. The monotonous and unpredictable patchwork of day and night continued. There was nothing clear about time, when my relationship to everything and everyone was absolutely unclear.

IN THE HANDS OF A MAN FIGHTING TO RECALL,
A BLANK PIECE OF PAPER IS FRIGHTENING.

My sister Shary says, "I was trying to get Vince involved with the Texas Brain Injury Association, and with other people who could help him, because I felt helpless. I had a very hard time dealing with his mood swings. Sometimes he would wake up in a rage, or if you did something that would piss him off, that was it. He was really violent. I remember being very embarrassed about that. But at the same time, I would always defend my brother. I knew that the head injury magnified a thousand times over what might be there to begin with. Our family is very intense; we're just all very intense people."

I also saw my sister Lana in these solitary times. "Vince was very different. His balance was not good, he sounded different because of his throat, and he didn't look the same. He still had a cane. He was very emotional—he'd just start crying, and you wouldn't know why. And there was a lot of anger there. He didn't like the cane, and he would get angry at having to use it. He was trying to push himself a lot, and you just had to go with it. If there were tears, there were tears; if there was anger, there was anger. It would pass and then everything would be fine. But that was hard to understand—the mood swings were difficult.

"I would remind him of things—what he was, what he did, and what he stood for in life. 'Remember this, Vince?' But he had no memory of it. There was a lot of, 'Well, you did this, and you did that.'

'I did?' 'Yeah, you did.' There were drastic changes. One day he was one way, the next day it was upside down. It was incredible. It was as if he was somebody else."

Mandy Mercier recalls, "Vince's speech therapist told me, 'Don't expect too much. Of course, we must always be hopeful.' But she worked constantly with people who just didn't make it back. She said, sincerely, that you don't always prefer life with brain injury over dying. Thank God Vince had enough left to come back, so he was truly one of the lucky ones, but still—to go through what he went through. I was really struck by how much courage that must have taken, just inner courage. He would learn one little bitty thing each day, and nobody else could tell he'd learned it—almost like when you first learn a musical instrument. You're not ready to play in front of people, and it's a solitary thing. Maybe one of the reasons he was able to come back was that he already had that discipline from learning the guitar the first time.

"I always had the feeling that if anybody could do it, Vince could. Or that he could certainly come a lot further back than he had at that point. The therapist explained that if you have that kind of brain damage, it can take you back to a level where you may have less impulse control. She said that it was almost like going to a lower order—a more primary, primal level. It would manifest itself in different ways in different people, but for Vince it was anger that he couldn't control. She said that was a classic physical symptom. She also said she had never seen a person be nicer or more tolerant than he could be."

I largely lived like a recluse, absorbed, perhaps trapped, by my persistence. I rarely went anywhere for entertainment. No movies, no sports events, no music, and no interests in anything other than getting better. I was also self-conscious about being in such pain all the time.

I got a shipment of oleander bushes from the mail-order plant farm, Burpee. The spade was biting for me now. My technique, while far from fail-safe, had improved. I planted the bushes in a perimeter along the fence of the large, windy backyard. It was awfully cold that year. An unpredictably late freeze killed them all a couple of days after I put every one of them in the ground.

There must have been 40 or 50 dead plants ringing the lawn along the fence, all crunchy, brown, and lifelessly stiff as the frigid wind whistled through them. A wooden box with iron latches that accompanied their shipment was all that remained of that investment. It ended up in Music School filled with an assortment of notebooks, thingamabobs, and guitar strings. Those bushes were a lot of well-intentioned work for no good result. I felt like I was jinxed.

YOU'RE COVERING GROUND ONLY TO FIND WHAT IS UNDERFOOT IS UNFAMILIAR.

Sometimes I would talk to people over the anonymity of the phone. I felt disenfranchised. Sometimes I would call a relative, or a friend, or the head injury group in Austin just to cry. Sometimes it was a relief to tell another human being about it. But I found that the head injury group was as hopelessly confused about the disaster we survivors had all suffered as was anyone else. It made me realize just how large and featureless a wasteland I was limping through.

Bob reflects, "I don't think Vince liked to go out in public. He'd go places where he was safe. I think he felt rather conspicuous. Some days would be real good for him, and then he'd have a setback of some kind and it would be frustrating for him to be around people. He did enjoy coming to see me at the Marina. Nobody expected him to do anything, no one knew him from Adam. No comparisons. He was just who he was. In those situations, he felt all right."

I spent the night at Bob's house. Early in the morning, the phone rang. Bob picked up the receiver and rolled his eyes as he spoke out of the corner of his mouth, "Nope, Chug won't be here till tomorrow. Here, hang this up would you?" He handed the remote to me and went back to the window facing out on Lake Travis. Grabbing a paper towel, he doubled it up on a plate on the counter. The smell of big, thick strips of bacon wafted about the early-morning kitchen.

I continued from my bar-stool perch, "So anyway, these days I just heel and toe into the mirror. Try to get the left foot to do like the right foot does. In the process, I'm ruining all of my s-shoes."

"That's good therapy despite the shoes, I bet. You hang in there."

"You know, I'm not so sure I will swim while I'm out here today. I can still drown in a glass of water, much less a lake."

Bob optimistically countered, "That's fine, 'cause we can always take the boat to the High Line marina and have a few beers instead."

"I remember l-liking to swim underwater, kinda," I drifted.

"I think you will again. Just don't give up."

As I cleared the sleep from my eyes, "Remember that storm that tore up the bar on the marina that summer? I played guitar there just before that. I was talking with someone in town the other day. They have never even been to Lake Travis."

"So, you want three or four pieces?" he asked.

"My favorite part is around Mansfield Dam near the L.C.R.A. park. I'd love some bacon. I remember that, kinda, from when I was kid. My parents and I stayed at a camp near the dam when I was very young."

"Well, then we'll go down to the marina today in the bass boat."

Between bites on a biscuit: "Me and my brother. And it was so hot, all the rocks looked flat and bleached right up to the water w-where a float was out from the shore that we swam back and forth from."

Bob dished up breakfast, "Eat up, and we'll go."

"You know, I actually don't taste this bacon. But I can taste the sweetener in this coffee. Could I have another cup?"

Bob finished washing the cast iron pan and eating before he even sat down, "Now, you sure you've had enough? I can always fry up more bacon."

"I lose things in my mouth these days," putting a napkin down. "Sometimes it makes me gag. Eating is one of my least favorite things to do. But thanks anyway."

"Hmf. We'll have lunch early today. They got a great hamburger down at the marina."

Me smiling, "I sure liked sleeping in the spring house. I like the ping-pong table the most. You gotta give me another shot at you today—my balance feels better than it did last night. Are we going to the marina? I need my sunglasses, have you seen my bag? Would you remind me to get some Vitamin C at the marina store, my arm hurts."

"If you're ready, we're outta here. I'm gonna lock it up while we're gone. Take this life vest to the boat, will you?" And then almost instantly, "Never mind, just put this other vest on over your shirt, I got the other one." Then to himself, "Now, where did Chug put the keys?"

Talking quietly all the while, I began to move jerkily down the floating dock from the white lake house with yellow trim to the bobbing and metallic-blue bass boat. "I'm trying to get off that rat bastard cane. So, I have to heel and toe because my big right toe sticks up. It won't be long before it puts a hole through the top of my shoe."

I crawled up into the front of the low-slung sliver of a boat on to a tall seat that swiveled 360 degrees, "That's why this is a new pair."

"Pardon?" as he tossed a tether into the boat and turned the outboard over again.

"... of shoes," I explained. Then forgetting myself yet another time, "What do you think about going to the marina?"

> LONELY WAR, QUIET VICTORIES.
> THE GREATEST DUEL IS WITH SILENCE.
> LIFE AFTER DEATH IS A TERRIBLE JOKE.
> CAN YOU OVERCOME LONELINESS?

YOU ARE ONE OF A KIND. I'M NOT GOING TO HOLD
    THAT AGAINST YOU.
IT'S LIKE MEXICO CITY IN HERE. I DON'T KNOW
    ANYONE AND I DON'T SEEM TO SPEAK THE
    LANGUAGE.

One day I went to a brain injury group meeting back at Bracken-ridge Hospital. A neurosurgeon was talking desperately about his newly head-injured son. Even he didn't know what to do after viewing the chilling depths of the condition. I never attended a meeting after that. It broke my heart to see such clever people lost for alternatives to that devastation. Staying busy, staying occupied, was my salvation in these times when a good thought was my closest companion.

There were no more doctors. My faith was firmly in myself now, for better or for worse. No one else on Earth could tell what was wrong with me better than I. No one else could effectively implement the never-ending treatments I required. I had played along for a year doing the treatments prescribed for me, and had seen eight doctors and several therapists every week. To their credit, they got me started in the right direction. But outrage and hardship loomed into every morning sky. My fears were great that if I couldn't whip this brain injury, no one could. I would walk through airports. I would talk as clearly as a telephone operator. I still dreamed of music.

I never worked harder on any cinder-block toting job, or in digging postholes and stringing fence wire in the sweltering deep woods of East Texas than I did now. But instead of being a pissing contest for good pay, this was an exacting dance of mental calculation and physical tedium.

The tools I required, my arms, legs, and vocal cords, had been broken and were rebuilt or different. Things had to be figured in advance for my limited abilities. I could do a particular drill too much, making the new muscles in the rebuilding arm too tired. That meant I got less good work done that day, and that led to more monotonous hours in workout hell. The figuring of my homespun exercise program was extraordinarily time-consuming. The refinements to the program occurred throughout its duration and were a feature of its usefulness. I had to be clever in my judgment of an injury, its resulting shortcoming, and its solution. Thinking about it well, I could conjure the proper adjustment of repairing treatments. The trick was to know when to adjust, yet be wary enough to know that most conditions could change tomorrow. Most did on a regular basis.

> I'M CURIOUS TO KNOW WHERE THIS KIND OF
>   BRAVERY COMES FROM.
> A HERO IS JUST A MAN WITHOUT A CHOICE.
> YOUR GIFT IS THAT YOU ARE RELENTLESS.

Bob Sturtevant says, "Vince was on a mission to put his life back together again and to try to find ways to enjoy himself, ways to have something about his life that was not burdened by his injuries. His emotions were still out of whack, even a year a half later. Many times when I was working on his house, he'd follow me out to the front porch and tears would be running down his face as he'd wave good-bye to me. These emotions were out of proportion.

"He was very concerned about getting normal. He said, 'You know, people don't want to see you coming home limping. Nobody likes to see that.' There were a lot of sober, direct remarks about his determination to beat this thing.

"And through all that he maintained an anger that just seethed. He seethed for a long time. In fact, I think that there is a part in him that is still seething. He's pissed off. And rightly. But he's channeled his seething into a determination to go on with his life. Maybe the fury has turned into some sort of a fuel."

I JUMPED OFF THE EDGE OF THE WORLD.
I WILL BE ANGRY TILL THEY SHOVEL ME UNDER, FOR
  GOOD.
HAVE YOU THE STRENGTH TO REBUILD?
I AM INTENSE AND UNFORGIVING.

I knew that the only thing that beat one good day of work toward my goals was two. So I trudged onward into the blackness of 1984. I counseled patience to myself while trying to control my unpredictable and excessive temper. Channeling the nervous energy I possessed was demanding, for now it was energy that had no familiar place to go. I was a stranger to myself except in the Black Book. But I was delighted to be corralling what ideas I could in the book. It gave a soothing texture to the dimness of my life.

♪　*XXII*　♪

Monday for Two Years

I bought assorted fruit trees from that same plant company later in the year, thinking that I was doing well enough to give growing something outdoors a chance again. I ordered $150 worth. When they arrived, I put them behind the front door until I could plant them. They wouldn't fit anywhere else conveniently because they were so tall.

I forgot they were behind the door almost immediately. They were gone from my recollection and I didn't find them for months. They died from lack of water, their plastic shipping packages still tied around the roots in a shriveled bundle. My disappointment at their ruination was tempered by the vagueness I was living in. A year later, I ordered another shipment of trees. The same thing happened. After that I made sure I lost that catalog.

My voluntary and treeless solitude at Music School made most people uncomfortable. They were either overwhelmed or dispassionate about the drama that I was living. It was easier to ignore me, even though I was desperately shouting at the top of my lungs, paralytic vocal cords notwithstanding. I was not clamoring for their sympathies. I needed something much dearer and far more difficult to give: their understanding. What I didn't realize at the time was that they didn't know how to react to someone who's died and then been brought back brain- and nerve-damaged. They suffered a "confusion of kindness." Or they just nervously turned around and walked the other way. Or they didn't say the right things, or do the right things. Often these were the closest of friends, sometimes a concerned family member, but they shied away because it hurt to watch me.

As I had quite rightly figured, no friend of mine wanted to see me come limping. They wanted to see me as they had before: "young, drunk, and hot to go." There wasn't a lot of that Vince left, and I was afraid of letting anyone who had known me before see me like this. As a result, I never found myself chumming it up with my music buddies from the past. Most of my old friends treated me like a tragedy, like the walking dead. In self-defense I rarely thought of yesterday. It hurt to be so different from the people I had shared a career with.

> I WISH THE WORLD WASN'T GOING SO FAST IT HAD
>   TO LEAVE ME BEHIND.
>   LIVING WITH THE UNDEAD.

The most comforting thing I came to know about people who view a serious-injury condition is that they are just people. They run like hell from things they don't understand. No one understood me or my cockeyed little world now.

For the record, it's easier to lie in the sickbed. When you stand at the side of one, you open a whole other can of worms. I will always have great affection for the courage of my closest friends and relatives. They had to watch my uncontrollable slide into brain damage. It was like I was balanced on the edge of a black hole, and no one was prepared to endanger themselves by lending me a hand. I couldn't blame them, and I couldn't forgive them.

No one could help because they didn't know how. If I was to walk or talk easily, or to play the guitar, I'd have to show them. This concept was as important to know about the new world I was living in as anything else I would teach myself.

Kathleen Vick says, "He was hurt. I think there was an almost childlike surprise at the things that people would or wouldn't do. Just a genuine, hurt kind of surprise that people would react to him the way they did."

I had apprenticed myself to a local designer to see if I could perform the functions of a graphic artist. There I became familiar with T squares, Exacto knives, ink pens, and rubber cement. There I showed up on time and ran errands. All my musical friends used the same commercial artist, as had I in the years before. When they stopped by now, I tried to remain as scarce as I could.

While I was working there, I applied for funding from the state. After some spirited horse-trading on my part, the Texas Brain Injury Association agreed to send me to Austin Community College to study commercial art. At first they had suggested, "We'll get you a job at a 7-11 or a shoe store or we'll send you to school." Convincing them that an art degree would be something the brain injured could accomplish was my first piece of artwork before the classes even began. After considerable wrangling over careers, test scores, and aptitudes, our conversation ultimately boiled down to just what it was that I wanted to do with the rest of my life. No doubt they found me as affable as had the physicians with whom I had been acquainted.

> THE ARTIST IN ART SCHOOL.
> I WORKED FOR OVER A YEAR AND A HALF JUST TO
>   EARN A HANDICAPPED PARKING STICKER.
> I FEEL LIKE I COULD SAVE EVERYONE ON BOARD BUT
>   MYSELF.

DAMN I'M TRYING.
YOU CAN'T LOOK TOO HARD FOR YOUR DREAM. OR
  CAN YOU?

In May, I spruced up and went off to school with a bag of art supplies, courtesy of the state of Texas. I started to pursue a commercial
art degree plan at ACC. My thoughts of further education were bit-
tersweet, but school was somewhat of a relief. I was effectively dead
to anyone who had ever known me. Now I just wanted to fit in somewhere. I was getting a fair return on my never-ending efforts to regain
the ability to walk and talk, but progress was slow. I remained unable
to do much on my own away from Music School. It began to look
like I would need that handicap sticker on that old van of mine for
the rest of my days. I viewed college as I never had before. Perhaps a
role I could play in another career would turn my little boat around, I
thought. I ached for a tailwind. I was still willing, if not so able.

If I was going to school, I was going to give it my best. At the same
time, I kept up the work in music because I was not willing to sacrifice
the song in my life. From the backseat, the pressure I felt to get back
into the musical performance fray lessened. I was even able to dig
deeper and harder into my music training, learning my craft better
than before, because of the unhurried pace I could now afford.

I never confused the two disciplines, education and avocation.
One would get meticulously reported in the Black Book. The other
would come back to me from class with a grade. School was serious
business, but music was a life-sustaining reason to believe in myself. I
loved them both for what they were to me. I gratefully found that one
would teach the other rather well.

I still could not pronounce many words. I couldn't speak without some
stranger knowing I was head-injured or thinking I was drunk. From the

hospital attendants earlier to my professors now, my privacy was zero. It was like I was some poor, unfortunate fool who had a stone collar around my neck that signified, "Hi, I'm a Traumatic Brain Injury Survivor." I never saw the people I met at school away from class. Ever. I guess I was pretty spooky to those folks, not talking above a whisper and walking like a freak-show Frankenstein's monster on a cane.

As school continued, I kept teaching myself how to say the words and phrases like "thousandth," "Washington," "small change," "exactly," "already done" and "big-league potential." I just couldn't seem to spit them out. I practiced saying words like these all the time between school assignments, daily voice exercises, and music rehearsal. After countless repetitions they became second nature, or as close to that as it was going to get.

"Vince had a lot of insecurity about everything," says Bob Sturtevant. "I mean, here was a man who didn't even know when he was hungry. The only time he realized he was hungry was when he felt better after eating lunch."

> I CAN'T REMEMBER WHEN I LAST ATE.
> IT'S STILL TOUGH TO NOT TASTE.
> USED A MIC FOR THE FIRST TIME HALLOWEEN '84.
> NOVEMBER '84, I WALKED WITHOUT A CANE.
> IT'S BEEN MONDAY FOR TWO YEARS.
> I STARTED PUSHING SOME AIR ON 11/16/84.

On that cane, I had successfully negotiated several school buildings full of UT dropouts and belated 35- to 60-year-old ancients like myself. I had an easier time keeping my balance in the supermarket as a result. Because I attended my lessons well and passed my courses, I could calculate all manner of day-to-day life with newfound security. Most important, I could speak better after using the voice I had labored over to communicate with all those school kids and their teachers. Every semester I could be proud of something, for the first time since Christmas 1982.

At Music School I played my old song "Sun & Moon & Stars" for the first time in September, and the song "Mirror, Mirror" showed up on my desk after I toyed with the idea from some Black Book passages. "Mirror" was an important story about the absolute aloneness I felt in the necessary isolation of Music School. Learning who you talked to when you needed to talk and you didn't travel beyond the walls of your living room was a profound experience. Away from the classroom, the only person I seemed to have anything at all in common with, or who had any interest in me, was my reflection in the glass.

I was so grateful for that.

I booked a show at Anderson Fair on December 21. Tim Leather-wood arranged for me to perform on that shadowy second anniversary of my wreck, twisted synapses and all. Years before, I had helped buy the air conditioning for the Fair with proceeds from the beer and wine sales from my evenings when I was a top bill. This year, I needed the favor returned.

The date scared me. It was my first foray out into the real world, back at an old haunt filled with the ghosts of yesterday, and I was beside myself in preparation. I had ratcheted myself up for this one, preparing to play many of the songs I had always performed, with a scattering of the new ones for good measure. I wanted the world to know that I wouldn't be kept down and that my future works would be all the talk, just as the older ones had been. By the sound check for the evening, though, I was prepared for the worst.

That night I played my damnedest on the familiar old stage that now felt like the pinnacle of a mountain top. My balance deserted me completely. Nothing was the same as it had been in rehearsal. I wasn't comfortable with my equilibrium for a moment. My poise was painted all over my face but never ran further than skin deep. I just couldn't concentrate. I made it through by being determined, relentless, and resolute, just like at home. That was as discouraging a result of my hard work as anything had been for two years.

I bit down hard and never gave up. I hoped no one would know just how bad it was for me. Wave after wave of imbalance plus piecemeal coordination in my hands and feet left me bewildered as I played the familiar old songs. My partially paralyzed vocal cords wandered uneasily through the themes. The performance was mercifully over about one o'clock that morning.

After two sets of material, I was exhausted, just like in the old days. At least that was the same, I thought to myself. Whatever insecurities people saw that night were unbeknownst to me, for I was too busy playing just like I had practiced.

"I was there, and it was really hard," Shary says. "I cried. I was horrified and depressed. It was horrible. Vince was a mess, and it was hard to see, because I had always been so proud of him."

On the drive back to Austin the next day, I considered whether I had seen my last night of performance. Regardless of the most generous light I could shine on it in the stark, cool glare of a southwestern winter's day, I felt that night had beaten me like a drum. I thought to myself, You can't give up, you turkey. It's not your way. Buck up, pal. I drove home to pick up my dogs for the quiet Christmas celebration at my parents' house in the East Texas woods a few days later. I was very glad that I was in school.

SUN & MOON & STARS

The sun and moon and stars
make the wind blow.
Took me twenty years
to understand.

Lost to me is how the lives
of friends go.
Like autumn leaves
in Oklahoma wind.

It made me strong,
to be on my own.
It never did me no harm,
to live all alone.
But, now and then
in the color of the evening,
drunken in a bar room,
with the fan turning,
I come to miss a few.

This afternoon was cloudy
and the rains came.
Third day of my first stay,
San Miguel.
Seems lately as I'm doubling
as storm bait,
been followed like a shadow
since the Dells.

Dear friendships and relations,
see what I have done.
I gathered all my fingers in one place.
They breathe a breath
that's deathly stale
since they tooled a song for me.
Guess mechanics never really set the pace.

Keep Your Eyes in the Sky

*T*he night at the Fair was as sobering as the air-conditioning bill in summer. It kindled intensely private fires in me that over the next years I kept well under wraps. Though a feeling of urgency incinerated me, I would contain my desire to again live the life I once sacrificed everything for. I could hold onto the dream. In my heart of hearts, I knew it wouldn't let me down. This was an acceptable, perhaps necessary, counterpoint to the hurricane that was blowing in my head night and day. This storm of grave disappointments and the harshest of realities was beyond me. Until it blew itself down to gale proportions, I would remain at its mercy.

It probably helped the staggeringly slow pace of my life along to have these titans waging constantly in me. When one threatened to blow me away, the other would give hope if I could hold on. As a result, the rest of my college career was punctuated by new songs, performance dates, and recordings in juxtaposition to this strange new career that I was dutifully preparing for. I still hoped each musical performance would be a little more encouraging than the last and give me a sign that music could again be my real career.

"Vince and I had a life-drawing class together," remembers my basil-growing friend Franci. "Art school was good for Vince because it slowed him down. The drive to do music never went away, but he diverted himself with school, and it ate up three years. It gave him something to focus on and do. But he never lost sight of the playing."

The resource I appreciated the most in 1985 was time with my buddies the beasts. I was alone with my animals for much of time that year when I wasn't attending a class. We'd watch TV side by side, mesmerized kitties and me. My felines would raptly follow the birds that soared across the color screen in those *National Geographic* PBS specials. When the herds of water buffalo grunted, or the nostrils flared on the hippopotami sinking into the river, the cats twitched and eagerly shifted their weight from one paw to the other. Their eyes never left the screen. They appeared no less interested when the show would dissolve to the expressionless and droll pledge-drive host.

Buffy, the aging, blue-gray Australian heeler, and I would play with a Frisbee out in the yard before sunset. The dog had a curly tail. I loved that cattle dog more than most of the people I had ever known. Our history had been a long one. We had traveled together for many years between the clean snowfalls of the Sierra and the soaking rains of San Francisco Bay to the filthy slush of New York City when the trees of Central Park were leafless and heavy with ice.

Twelve-pound Pup, a Wizard of Oz-looking little dog, came to me wild from the woods around Bastrop, Texas. That fuzzy little mister would scale the chain-link fence at Music School in a heartbeat, like a seasoned rock climber. He roamed the neighborhood for several streets around like a representative of the property owner's association.

My conversations with these best of buddies were some of my most important. Regardless of how tough it was and how hard circumstance came down, they cared for and needed me. I cared for and needed them. They never looked at me with anything but love, from the initial day I came home in 1983 looking like a chatty cadaver. They counted on me for love, canned cat food, and pooch noodles. My reward was they never failed me. I never failed them.

But, the world was not standing still and neither was I.

My old music-colleague-turned-lawyer, David Rodriguez, dropped by from time to time with Brian Ferry and Lou Reed tapes for me to peruse. I thought that was novel. I was being exposed to music by my friend the barrister. He never stayed very long, but he tried to bring me some of the world I didn't go out to see much anymore. We found time to coauthor a song. He did the music, and I provided the lyrics.

In March, after starting my first English composition class in over a decade, I enthusiastically took a job performing on a bill with Joe Ely at Rockefeller's, a Houston concert hall. The chance to make good again was what I lived for.

The building housing the club was the former Heights State Bank on Washington Avenue, just north of Buffalo Bayou and west from the downtown concentration of 50-story skyscrapers. The green room and backstage was the former bank vault with walls several feet thick.

Joe and I had known of each other through the local music grapevine. It was a joy to talk during sound check. We were veterans of some of the same roadhouse barrooms scattered all over Texas. Playing in the elegant former foyer of an ex-bank was pretty hip and fancy compared to those bygone roadhouses.

We both played solo with acoustic guitars. It was a pleasure. No amplifiers, no kick drums, no distortion boosters, no spangled jackets, just the guitars and the guts. They put a stool up under the microphone and filled the room with warm bodies. We two veterans of those Texas brawlrooms knew well what to do. We looked out from the richly carpeted stage into the darkness of the marble-floored room and saw fluted chairs around glass-topped cocktail tables crowded with interested smiles. Large, kidney-shaped balconies waved around the edges of the main floor. Tasteful modern paintings and elegant sculptures clung to the colored walls.

We held court for four hours that evening, my openers to his feature shows. There were polite calls for encores from the satisfied clientele and congratulations all around. We earned our pay when the club came away with good cover charges at the door. Drinks sold like hot cakes that night.

Joe said, while we were packing up to leave, "You know, we know many of the same people." I hadn't had the kind of conversation that ensued in several years. For a few hours that evening, my Panhandle performing partner made me recall some of why we had started encoring in the first place. But it was years before that club would ask me back.

> DON'T TELL ME THE PARTY'S OVER, I JUST GOT HERE
>   AND BROUGHT MY FRIENDS. THEY THINK I KNOW
>   YOU.
> AW, CAN'T YOU JUST PRETEND.
> I'M NOT TALKING INDEPENDENCE. I'M TALKING
>   LONELINESS.

Meanwhile, back at English composition class, the local poet got a C.

At Music School, the coffee pot would shudder into operation about six o'clock every morning, and the daily routine of serious rehabilitation would continue while I passed course after college course through the spring of 1987. I would work on the floor or at a drafting table to finish art projects, sweating and cussing in the abominable Texas heat with the ceiling fans slowly turning. In the next moment, I would shed the shirt and don a pair of gym shorts for the exercises.

IT TAKES THESE TEARS TO MAKE A CHAMP.

It was the leanest of times for making and keeping friends. Companionship was terribly important to someone who tried so hard to ignore closeness and who had so little confidence in feeling "normal." Only my own best efforts were going to get me better, and that didn't have anything to do with filling a social calendar. My attitude was very self-sufficient and proud. I worked myself harder than I had been worked by any vocal or physical therapist. Before the mental institution, I might have been accused of being a little crazy; I now had papers.

> I'VE BEEN LOOKING FOR MS. RIGHT. NOW, I JUST
>   WANT TO FIND MS. RIGHTNOW.
> I JUST WISH SOMEONE WOULD LOVE ME FOR NO
>   DAMNED GOOD REASON.
> IT'S IMPORTANT TO FEEL YOU CAN HIT BOTTOM
>   AND SOMEONE WILL STILL LOVE YOU. IT MAKES
>   YOU TRY FOR THE BRASS RING.
> YOU KNOW YOU'VE BEEN HERE A WHILE WHEN YOU
>   NEED TO TAKE A BATH AND CAN'T REMEMBER THE
>   LAST.

The revolving door's worth of girlfriends during the tedious years of my reeducation were to teach me some of my hardest lessons. Some were extremely kind. Some were not worth the horrible inconveniences they brought. None stayed. By the time I was through with school, I was through revolving. Ms. Rightnow was nowhere to be found.

> SUCH BEAUTY IN HER FINGERTIPS. SUCH UGLINESS
>   IN HER HEART.
> THE WAY I KNOW HOW IMPORTANT THE SONGS ARE IS
>   THEY'RE STILL GOOD WHEN THE GIRL'S GONE.
> COMFORT IS TO BE ABLE TO REACH DOWN FOR
>   ANYTHING.
> HAVING TO REACH UP ALL THE TIME IS TIRING.

In April of 1986, I backed into my next performance opportunity. School was winding down, I was passing all my courses and taking one of my final production art classes. I no longer used a cane or stuttered or drooled. I chatted with people along the way. From time to time, I stopped by the department office to say hello to the secretary or the department head. I was a regular gadfly.

We all took our seats on stools behind the drafting tables as our professor, Sam Richardson, explained that he had been contracted to do the poster for an event at the Austin Opera House, a place I had encored at several times in the before life. It was to be called the "April Fool Off." It featured Alex Harvey and other notables and was part of the state of Texas's sesquicentennial celebrations.

In a time now long past, I had played several nights around the Austin area with Alex Harvey. The last time was at a place called the Alamo Roadhouse. We paced back and forth in our bone-chilling back room. Shivering, Alex said, "You and I, we're c-crazy to be here, but no one else could do this . . . you know?"

Back in that stuffy spring classroom I said, "Tell Alex I would like to be on that bill." I immediately shrunk back into my chair. Sam replied, with an eyebrow raised, "I sure will," and went back to his lecture.

Next week he told the class, "This is the artwork I added to the poster this weekend. Do you see how I stacked the names of the musicians down the center of the page rather than in one of the gutters on the sides? The typeface is 16-point Bodoni and oh, by the way, Vince, Alex says you're on. This arrangement helps the reader . . ."

When I arrived just after dark at the familiar stage door of the Opera House, my mind raced into yesterday. It had been a long time since I had seen the place. I set my guitar case in one of the back rooms at stage side, then walked into the hot, white fill-lights being adjusted by the light man from his projection booth behind the rounded rows of theater seats.

The stage lights came up an hour later. I was one of the first to play that night, and one of the names farthest down the list on the poster, but I couldn't have been prouder. The host was none other than dapper Sam Richardson, in tux and tails. He did all the introductions, including my own. Hobnobbing with the other musicians was the high point for me in 1986. There were 17 acts, from Mickey Newberry to Asleep at the Wheel. I knew half a dozen of the performers well.

In class the next week, Sam presented me with a plaque from the state that read, "In appreciation for outstanding contribution, exceptional showmanship, and Texas-size entertainment in celebration of the 150th Birthday of the Lone Star State." It was signed by the Speaker of the Texas House of Representatives, a member of the Texas Senate, and the Secretary of the Senate. The Texas state seal in gold leaf with draped flags and a ribbon of red finished out the framed memento. I put it on the wall at Music School across from my desk. I would feel better about myself every time I glanced over at it while in the midst of some horrible exercise that year.

Sam remembers the semester, "I first met Vince when he enrolled in one of my commercial art courses at Austin Community College. Those were the golden days of the boogie in the roach-clip-key-chained, we-don't-need-no-stinkin'-badges Austin music scene, where the rednecks and the hippies got together and made music history. And Vince was a big part of it.

"But his time at ACC represented a little detour on his loop around Austin's city limits. My job at the college was to try and teach people something about design and typography and how to get 'art' ready for the printer, skills that might earn them a paycheck. It was more craft than art but graduates of our program were better prepared for the real world than art grads who matriculated from the big university across town with their cute little portfolios of abstract expressionist splatter and watercolored sunsets.

"Vince was a good student: dedicated, diligent, and humble. Dedicated to improving himself and, as I learned later, healing himself, diligent in his work ethic, and humble because he knew how fragile life is. And he was glad to be a part of our program. He was glad to be part of anything. And he'd decided that the negative alternative was not an option and told bad luck to take a hike.

"So Vince started on the long road back to his career and to his life. He enrolled at ACC to learn a new trade, just as a backup in case his musical powers didn't come back, and he did well in his studies. But he did better in his rehab, and people who are entertained by Vince today, people who don't know his story, might never guess that the troubadour with the raspy voice and the thoughtful, measured lyrics took a trip to hell and back one time.

"Teachers sometimes inspire students, but in Vince's case, it was the student who inspired his teacher."

I graduated a two-year degree program in three years, magna cum-later than most, but what I had started leaning on a cane, I finished walking upright.

I had expected that my condition would have improved significantly by now. So much for assumptions. The toes on my left foot would still bind painfully without strict attention. My gait was halting and uneven, requiring constant training at the running trampoline every afternoon. Words would get caught up in my throat while I jogged: "Nine thousand nine hundred and six, nine thousand nine hundred and seven . . ." in time with the left footfalls. I didn't rest well, or sleep very long. I still cried a lot.

My right arm would swell and was very painful from day to day. Only taking massive amounts of vitamin C would alleviate the agony. I came to believe that my body considered the girder-shaped metal piece that replaced the bone in my right forearm a foreign object. If my arm could speak, I imagined it would say, "Hey pal, make no bones about it. What's this doin' in here?" My arm would get infected from time to time as my body tried to excise the offending material. Once in a while, I would pick up something too heavy and exceed the tensile strength of the metal. Like an eye-watering, wrenching wakeup call from the past, it would bend somewhat. The lightning stab of pain I felt helped me to recall what not to do next time I felt like pulling some Herculean feat. And I could still drown in that glass of water.

These were the conditions of survival now. That was just the way it was and perhaps would always be. The only mistake I could make about these alterations was to fear them. My salvation lay in whatever powers I could summon that would allow me to rise above them and go on with my life.

I'M PRIVILEGED TO SHARE THE TEARS WITH YOU.
IT'S BEEN SO LONG, IT'S GOING TO BE LONGER.
SO, WHEN WILL THE CRYING STOP?

♪ *XXIV* ♪

Second Street

School had been a great diversion. It was the most patience-testing activity I could ever have dreamed of. It kept me more constructively busy than anything else I had subjected myself to. It sharpened my thoughts like a blade. And the next diversion was on its way. I began running a musical lounge show out of the State Theater, a rundown Triple-X movie house in downtown Austin, two blocks from the pink granite state capitol building and next door to the storied, long-lived Paramount Theater and the Driskill Hotel.

My idea was to present live music in the lobby at night. If I couldn't do the stand-up comedy-music show I used to do, maybe I could front a group and leave some of the entertaining to the drummer, the bassist, or the other guitar player in my new band.

I invited some friends to put together a couple of months of entertainment. My new band played. Butch Hancock and Jimmie Dale Gilmore played one weekend. Steven Fromholz brought his best old Martin, named Leonard, and illuminated an evening or two. A popular College Station band, the Side Effects, brought old buddies, harmonica-playing Doug Duryea and violinist Ellen Moore. Shake Russell played. Ray Wylie Hubbard cameoed one evening after coming all the way from Dallas.

All in all it was a flop, but if they'd given awards for spirit, we'd have received Oscars.

I continued to rehearse my band there but, not unexpectedly, I lost my key to the unusual space after a year. Before I left the place for good, I ran a songwriters' showcase out of the State for South by Southwest, a music and media conference. On that evening, I put 14 acts onstage for three or four songs apiece. Running the show again was trying. Attempting to stay roughly on schedule and giving everyone the opportunity to be heard was as thankless a job as I had undertaken. By the time the night was done, I retired from music promotion. My future was obviously not in the hosting or sponsorship end of the entertainment industry.

Bob Sturtevant says, "Vince had put a band together. He'd started playing piano again, and he did a few songs on the piano in the concerts. His voice wasn't anywhere near where he wanted it, and he wasn't satisfied with that. He looked at it as a big drawback at the time. But he had something going, and they got out there and they did it. He knew it wasn't what he wanted to do, but he was doing something. And it seemed to be part and parcel of his ongoing Music School."

I lost my brother Gary in March.

> "LIFE'S HIGHWAY IS THE ONLY ROAD YOU'LL FIND
> FAR TOO LONG AND YET FAR TOO SHORT."
> —GARY BELL, MARCH 1987

My education completed and a reintroduction to the trials of music over, I began to seek employment. After a thorough but unsuccessful look into the design field, my desperation grew. Finding work at the age of 35 was going to be chancy at best, and it didn't help one bit for me to be head-injured. Could I remember what I was told? Could I remember the day of the week? Or where I put the car? Where were my keys, my wallet?

Everything I did was still being figured out to the nth degree in advance. My support systems were simple, direct, and designed to be foolproof and unpressured. Working in the real world would be spontaneous. Entering the structured working world was no way like attending classes or performing a set of music. With this in mind, I approached Goodwill Industries through the ever-helpful Texas Rehabilitation Commission.

Goodwill assigned me to be a floor clerk in Round Rock, 20 miles north of Austin just off my favorite Interstate 35. For several months, I folded and displayed used clothing on the racks of their thrift store in a pleasant outdoor shopping center. I accepted donations from the local housewives, swept floors, squeegeed windows, and stacked boxes in the back of the shop. It was gratifying to learn that I could do a day-to-day job without my injuries affecting my performance. But I wanted to do more than this.

My next move was to go down to the infamous Second Street to find a construction job. I reasoned that I could make a difference using the muscle in my good arm. Second Street was where the desperately unemployed or homeless went to earn a day's wage from construction contractors who were looking for contract labor minus the taxes and insurance. It was a cultural phenomenon as much as an economic one. When I showed up two hours before daybreak, there was already a mob milling around under the street lamps' bluish glow. The individual huddles of shadowy men silhouetted by the occasional yellow flash of matches formed walls of different languages and unintelligible conversations, mostly in Spanish.

I was a minority of one standing by myself that cold, dark morning before dawn. The earliest rush-hour traffic was trickling by. An aging pickup truck rounded the corner and slowed to a stop just under a lamp.

We clamored together around the sidewalk side of the truck. A tall, white man in a cowboy hat popped the manual stick shift out of gear, set the emergency brake, and emerged from the well-lit cab in one fluid movement with his eyes focused on a clipboard in his hand, and announced, "I'm looking for four warm bodies to haul brick all day long," with the emphasis on "all, day, long." "I'm paying 20 dollars in cash, I'm buying lunch, and I'm bringing you right back here when we're done."

"How 'bout you? (motioning to the big Salvadoran).

"And you (one of his buddies).

"And you (a large, round man called Guerro).

"How 'bout it, pal? (motioning to a strong-looking kid who spoke English from east Austin who had given me a light).

"Anybody else? C'mon now, it won't kill ya."

We all jostled, "Hey, mister," and waved.

"No, not you, old man (to the only obvious wino staggering forward).

All right, that's it. You guys jump in the back of the truck, I'm stopping for coffee on the way."

Off the somber and sleepy-eyed chosen rode, for a day's worth of sweating off last night's Mexican beer on some barren and shadeless construction site in the suffocating Central Texas sun.

Back in "The Hotel" parked a block away, I sat for a silent minute, my head in my hands and my elbows on the steering wheel. I wasn't big enough, I thought. Maybe he could tell I was head-injured by the way I looked at him. I mean, he looked right at me. I wondered why he didn't pick me. The sun was just coming over the freeway in the east now. It was going to be another hot one. Perhaps I would try again tomorrow. Perhaps not.

SECOND STREET

The weary work for food
out in the Lone Star State.
Talking in tongues about tropical girls,
down on Second Street.
Where the living is hard.
Longer horns on that Mercedes Benz
might you never see.
Well-heeled Texana never tarries
down on Second Street.
Where the living is hard.
Austin, Texas, by the lake,
rich kids ski, legislators drink.
They huddle close against the cold,
down on Second Street.
Where the living is hard.
Tie a knot in that rope, hold on tight . . .

♪ *XXV* ♪

Fate Worse Than Death

*F*or five years I had not been able to re-
member where anything was unless I put it someplace where I would
routinely go every day to rediscover the things I would need. I had
introduced a support system that allowed me to keep track of everything I valued or needed. Consequently, my life was arranged into a
rotation of stations. There was a bowl for my wallet and keys at the
front door. In the piano room, the top of the dresser and the desk
served the same function for all music-related items: strings, tuners,
the Black Book, metronomes. In the kitchen there was a counter-
top for cutlery, a favorite plate, and a glass. All things that related to
school, including my driver's license and keys to "The Hotel," were
left on the drafting table or in the art bag I carried.

But I forgot to put things where they belonged so many times.
The indignity of losing something yet again drove me to fail-safe my
fragmented, piecemeal world as best I could. It's hard to describe the
disappointment I felt when I would turn around for the umpteenth
time and realize that I didn't know where my wallet and car keys were.
Often I could not tell if something was missing because I had forgotten about its existence. Like the poor trees behind the door of Music
School, some had paid for my forgetfulness with their lives.

Then came the black bag, the place I went to look for everything. The KISS principle was the order of the day: Keep It Simple Stupid. If it wasn't in the black bag, it didn't exist, because I probably couldn't remember what or where it was. I would carry this black bag everywhere. In it I kept pills, pens, pencils, a knife, a fork, and a spoon, a six-inch ruler, pads of paper, the Black Book, and chopsticks (?). There were scissors, paperclips, a pocketknife, hemostats, Band Aids, a fingernail file and clippers, a clock, a comb and brush, a flashlight, vitamin C, Ibuprofen, allergy medicine, and a box of matches. It was everything you might need in a black nylon, ripstop shoulder bag if you were shipwrecked and stranded on a desert island or in the middle of a large Midwestern city.

My next midnight foray into the working world was at the old Robert Mueller Airport, that same source of jet engine afterburn that I had been hearing from Music School for years. I inventoried parked cars for minimum wage on the graveyard shift. How appropriate. I made $3.95 an hour and felt lucky. The schedule would not interfere with my music reworking, especially since no one would have me playing in their joints. Again the "confusion of kindness" of others held my progress hostage. Best of all, no one would see me.

I arrived at work at 10:30 pm. I would lean my teardrop-shaped guitar case, still holding the Rich and not the Martin, and black bag against the temporary building that was the office and punch in on the time clock inside. Then I would throw the guitar and bag over my shoulders and walk down into a peripheral lot on the outskirts of the airport property. There at Booth 6, far apart from the rest of the airport, I would take over from the worker before me by doing a bit of paperwork and filling up my cash register with the standard amount of small bills and change. The booth was only big enough to hold one person at a time. Whether it was raining or freezing, I had to wait outside while the worker before me finished his or her calculations and exited the cubicle. It was glassed on three sides waist high. The rest of the construction was corrugated sheet metal. You can imagine the acoustics. There was a broken transistor radio on the steel counter and an electric heater in the wall. This booth was so remote from the others that it contained a Pullman-style bathroom. It suited me to be so far from anyone else.

> I LIKE BEING ALONE 'CAUSE THERE'S SO MUCH
>   WORK.
> IF I CAN BEAT THIS I CAN BEAT ANYTHING.

When the last straggling customers were gone, I would open my guitar case. The tiny booth was so small that I couldn't take the guitar out of the case and sit down in one movement. Sometimes it was just easier to place the stool outside in the rain and stand inside while I practiced.

One evening, an old acquaintance was the last to motor up to the booth. We had known each other a decade before when he and a great crowd of friends would come to see me play. At first he didn't recognize me. Stunned, I thought that was just as well as I looked away to the guitar standing at the ready just beneath the change window.

Then he chimed in, wide-eyed, "Vince, is that you?" I hid my shame in the smile I wore. He shoved his hand through the window and I responded by taking it as warmly as I could.

"Robert . . . so how have you been?"

"Just great. New babies and new cars, but more to the point, how the hell are you?"

"Getting by." I looked away, still smiling. I was dying inside. I never thought for an instant that I would run into anyone here who had known me. After a brief conversation punctuated with the typical "I thought you were a goner" and "Let me know if there's anything I can do" sentiments, he pulled away into the dark. I wanted to sink into the pavement. However, in ten minutes the pink in my cheeks was due more to the vocal scales than the waning embarrassment.

> YOU'RE A LONG WAY FROM THE CUTTING EDGE.
> DO, RE ,MI, FA, SO, LA, TI, DO, TI, LA, SO, FA, MI, RE, DO.
> GRIEVE AND WORK, GRIEVE AND WORK.

On another night, one of the airport shuttles pulled up to my booth and the young shuttle driver bounded from the front seat, the door left ajar. Knocking loudly at the window, he said with an anxious grin, "Mind if I use your restroom?"

"No, not at all." I mustered a smile to welcome the fellow as best I could and stood outside and whistled for a moment, while the radio in the van barked back and forth. In a short time he returned.

"You're Vince Bell, right?" he asked. "I saw an article about you in the paper a while ago. And wow, I can't believe what you've been through. Are you all right?"

"Yes, yes. I'm doing fine and better all the time. It's been a helluva trip so far, though."

We talked for ten minutes on company time like pirouetting dancers in our matching permanent-press shirts, slacks, and shoes. His honestly inexperienced questions and my honestly horrific answers intermingled under the glow of those crime-stopping yellow lights. He was kind, but there was no mistaking the patronizing tone in his voice. He was a youth, just coming of age, from the same east Austin neighborhood as the fellow who had run me over. "I don't think I could've done that," he said enthusiastically.

"You won't have to. Some other tragedy will confront you. Something that makes the bigness of your heart take over where nothin' else will do. Somethin' so big and so bad you can't even see all of it. It will demand the titan in you. That's life."

"Yeah, but . . ." he climbed a foot up into the bus.

"Don't worry, you won't find trouble . . . trouble will find you. Not when you're strong and looking for it. Believe in yourself. No one else will."

"Man, I'm glad to talk to you. You're an inspiration, and you're gonna be all right. I just know it. Gotta go. Thanks for the rest stop."

LIKE A LAWYER, MAKE A GOOD CASE AND THEN
DEPEND ON THE IGNORANCE OF THE JURY.

After checking out the last car leaving the lot, I secured the cash register and locked my guitar in the booth. Up and down, row upon row of vehicles, I walked for miles each night punching numbers and letters into a small keyboard. It took a couple of hours to make the rounds, and then I would hurry back to my guitar in Booth 6. The rehearsals there were as rigorous as the ones at Music School, only now they were in the middle of the night, and I was getting minimum wage to do them. Instead of running in place on the jogging trampoline, I circled the huge parking lots mindfully walking and loudly counting into the thousands during the hours of the dark early morning.

Inevitably, the sky would lighten. The chill of the night would lift, and it would become more humid. Cars would begin to filter in, and the shuttle buses would start their rounds. The first flights of the day took off in their usual deafening fanfare. That signaled the end of my night at the airport. I would trudge with guitar and black bag "up top," dodging rush-hour traffic with the sun just coming up in the east. After punching out, I would load up "The Hotel" and drive slowly out of the lot for home.

There the beasts would mob me, and we would joyously wrestle. I would collapse on the bed until the early afternoon. During the late afternoon, I would shop at the grocery store or wash clothes or work in the greenhouse. Sometimes I would call around to see if I could get myself into any music around town. But my searches turned up very little. Most of them would reply, "Vince Bell? Who are you? Oh, that's right, the guy that got run over. Howz it going? Let me know if there's anything I can do."

It was then that a musical production based on my story was performed. The two-act play was called *The Sun and Moon and Stars*, and included 18 of my songs as it journeyed through the story line of my accident. It was a small production with an eight-person cast, a musical director, a light man, and a costume designer. It premiered at the Dougherty Theatre in Austin. With my new graphic arts degree in hand, I produced the program and was listed as art director.

While I was pulling the nighttime shift, Bob Sturtevant introduced me to Tom Roudebush, who had a recording studio in his home in South Austin. We agreed to work together to complete the first Vince Bell album, which would also be called *The Sun and Moon and Stars*.

Bob says, "Vince was ready to go to the next step. And he needed to go to the next step. He still wasn't sure what was best for him to do. Should he go ahead and pursue music? It didn't seem like he was going anywhere. Vince and Tom hit it off, they put the album together, and it felt good."

I spent the better part of a year in Tom's studio recording.

Bill Browder, who had come in as music director for the project, recalls, "There were a lot of good ingredients there and Vince had made remarkable progress. There were several performances by him, and some arrangements, that were really good. I got a lot of positive feedback from people I would play it for, who said 'God, I didn't know Vince had come back that much.' There were some good creative things there."

Shary says, "I liked that tape, and I still play it occasionally. It's got one of my favorite songs on it—'Take My Chances with the Wind.' It was my first big ray of hope for Vince."

As my album was released on Tom's Analog Records to no great notice, I was forced to move to Houston to get the work I could not find in Austin.

Back in Houston, Tim Leatherwood and Nanci Griffith helped to breathe a little precious life into my lagging career when she decided to record my song, "Sun & Moon & Stars." These two people were deeply instrumental in my renaissance back into music. The move to Houston was refreshing, although I still was not welcome to perform my songs for anyone, old friend or not. The grievous reputation of my brush with fate died hardest of all.

I kept trying unsuccessfully to worm my way back into the mainstream of music. At the Fair and a club called Local Charm, in the dilapidated warehouse district around Telephone Road, I opened shows for old friends like Fromholz. I couldn't command any wage, so I usually did the support acts for nothing but exposure. I was lucky to get them, but it wasn't enough.

Music was still my reason for living, but no one would hire me to perform. Texas starved me out. I tried my heart out in several of its towns, but now I was forcibly introduced to a showbiz institution: reinventing myself. I had been dead in the water for almost a decade. I was damned if I was going to stay that way.

THE FATE WORSE THAN DEATH IS LIVING AGAIN.
    HOW DOES IT FEEL TO WALK THROUGH THIS WORLD
    WITH A TIGHT-LIPPED SMILE?

My last hurrah in Houston was to attend the wedding of one of my old high-school football chums at the posh River Oaks Country Club. I arrived from the "bad" side of town in the beat-up, bald-tired "Hotel." I pulled around the immaculately landscaped circle entrance in a long line of stylish automobiles. The parking-lot attendants politely opened the driver- and passenger-side doors simultaneously for each arriving couple. A ticket exchange later, the formally dressed guests would step onto the carpet leading to the opulent interior of the antebellum building. When my turn came to be pampered, I popped from "The Hotel" not quite as well dressed as the attendants and stuck out my hand for the ticket. With an imperious smile, the good fellow confided, "I don't think we'll need a ticket to find this one."

> BETTER TO HAVE TO JUSTIFY WHAT YOU'VE DONE
>   THAN WISH YOU HAD DONE IT.
> TO ALL THAT WALK THIS ROAD, HOLD ON, I'M
>   COMING.

♪ *XXVI* ♪

Wizard of Odds

YOU ARE THE WIZARD OF ODDS.
CRY TOUGH, BEAT THE ODDS.
LET'S GO AGAIN. I THINK I'M READY NOW.
TOMORROW TELLS THE TALE.

*O*n a hot and humid East Texas day in May of 1990 I drove to my parents' house in New Waverly. I pulled "The Hotel" up in the drive and walked quickly, without much of a limp at all, into the den. I sat down on the couch and faced my smiling but curious mother. I was a house afire. My jaw was set like charred foundation stone. I said, "Mom, I'm a songwriter, and I'm going out to live on Bob Sturtevant's front-room floor in Los Angeles."

She calmly replied, without a hint of surprise, "Good. I haven't heard that in you in a long time, Vince. Don't go without leaving us his number, would you?"

I had packed up "The Hotel" with just the essentials. I took the shirt on my back, the shoes on my feet, a trash can full of dirty clothes, and drafting table lights, as well as the black bag, my portfolio, and art bag with all the Rapidograph pens and rubber cement you could want, a microwave oven rotisserie cover, some extension cords, the two guitars and an amplifier on wheels, a music stand, a box of tools, a suitcase of unwound quarter-inch instrument cords and electrical adapters, two cassette machines and tapes, a phaser, a graphic EQ, a chorus ensemble, a digital delay, a microphone, a parametric EQ, a 200-watt amplifier, two speaker boxes the size of small refrigerators, a mic stand, a gold-plated bowling pin, a safari pith helmet, and a handful of cheap Mexican dirt-weed marijuana.

I thought it ironic that I had to go away to a mysterious part of the country in order to come back from the troubles that were dogging me.

The last entry in the Black Book read:

I THINK IT'S TIME TO RETIRE YOU, OLD BLACK BOOK.
     I'M GLAD TO LET YOU GO TO SOME DRAWER OR
     BOOKCASE WHERE YOU WILL BE SAFE FROM BAD
     MEMORIES, HARD MEMORIES, TOUGH THINGS TO
     CONFRONT. SO BE IT.
YOU'VE BEEN A HELLUVA COMPANION. I WISH YOU
     AND I, BOTH, THE BEST OF THE REST.
LUCK, COMPADRE.
P.S. LET ME FALL BETWEEN THE BEATS.

I had left the dogs with my mother, and I felt a little odd not having at least one sitting and panting in the rider's seat. I told myself I didn't care and stopped thinking about it. I knew the prices I would pay for every mile from here on out.

I hit Interstate 45 South, made a right on Interstate 10 West, and settled in for the long haul. The drive took as many hours as it takes to get there. I left my mother's couch and before I went to sleep, I was at Bob's door: Flatonia, Comfort, Sonora, Ozona, Madera Mountain, and Panther Mesa. I stopped for gas underneath Boracho Peak in the early dawn of the second day. The joke had always been, "It's a three-day ride to the kitchen in Texas." That morning, it didn't seem so extravagant a statement.

Cochise, Dragoon, Apache Pass—names crossed by history. Just west of Phoenix and just shy of sunset, I pressed a coin into a phone, and my spirits soared when Bob answered. I regaled him with my last 48 hours, and he suggested, "Don't you want to rest a little? Maybe get a room for the night?"

"I'll sleep when I'm dead. Now, about those directions when I get to L.A...."

The street lights for Los Angeles began 100 miles from town. I marveled at the retail run-amuck in all directions. It was exciting, bizarre, and invigorating at the same time. I had never seen so much cement molded into as much controlled confusion ever.

Six and a half hours after my call, it was 2:00 or 3:00 in the morning and I was sitting in Bob Sturtevant's pleasant, quiet, and warm breakfast room downing a glass of Scoresby Scotch with my best friend. Nothing vibrated. There was no wind or road noise. I was sunburned, dirty, and ready to begin my new life sleeping on that front-room floor. He said goodnight and I hit the deck next to the TV and the stereo.

I didn't dream.

For a month, I slept on Bob's floor in Altadena. I spent the time rehearsing guitar in a chair outside, facing the hedge around the backyard, and looking for odd jobs.

Bob recalls, "When Vince decided that it was time for him to come to California—his wild drive to the west—he took control of his life. He was prolific at that time, and it was a lot of fun to watch. He was working on four songs at once. It wasn't that he'd work on one and then put it down for two or three weeks. He was working on all four, in his head, at the same time. He was sleeping on the floor because I didn't have another bed, and I remember coming in a number of mornings and he'd be lying there, staring out into space, and writing the song in his head even before he got up for his first cup of coffee.

"Vince's convictions are the same today as they were in the beginning," says Bob. "He's a hearty soul. If Vince were any less of a person in his strength and his makeup psychologically, mentally, I don't know that he could have recovered from this accident. I know that he didn't cop out to drugs, he didn't cop out to anything. He got right back on the treadmill and had that discipline and that insistence that things go on. He has that to thank for being successful in his rehab."

Then fortune was good to me, and Sarah dropped back into my severely fragmented little world. "I had moved from L.A. to Berkeley," Sarah recalls. "Vince had gotten my phone number from a mutual friend. The phone rang on a Sunday in May, and we talked for a long time. It was the beginning of a many-week phone courtship."

One bright morning, as I emerged from the bath with a towel around my waist, Bob motioned to me, "Someone named Mike Walters just called you from the Virgin Islands. He was talking about you coming to play there in a couple of weeks."

"Pardon?" I was incredulous. If the towel had fallen down to my ankles I wouldn't have noticed. I dialed the number and got Mike, the brother of an old music-writing friend of mine from Houston, Sean Walters. "So Mike, howz it going?"

He reminded me of a conversation we'd had in a Texas bar a few months before. Now he said he had five weeks of gigs lined up on St. Croix. His business partner there, an islander from St. Martin named Fitz, was prepared to advance the money for my airline ticket. Mike closed by telling me, "The tickets will come by mail to your friend's. You can stay at my house near the salt pond. Gotta go. Sorry, the charge is running low on this remote phone. See you real soon."

I put the receiver back in its cradle, then silently walked to the glass doors that led to the backyard. My elation lasted for a week.

Two weeks later, Bob and I pulled into LAX late in the evening. I was carrying both guitars, a large duffel bag of clothes and music-related gear including black, tubular-metal guitar stands. The ever-present black bag was slung over my shoulder. When I hefted the baggage to the security conveyor, the tram jerked to a stop with my things under the X-rays. The security cop on duty standing by said suspiciously, "What are those long, metal-looking things?"

I said to Bob under my breath with obvious exasperation, "Oh, brother, he thinks they're disguised Israeli machine guns." As disarmingly as I could, I said, "Those? Those are just guitar stands . . . for the guitars." I pointed to the tear-drop and violin-shaped cases.

"I'm sorry, Mr. Bell, two bags only on this flight."

I could feel myself sinking. I needed the two instruments. That was the plan I had gone over and over again in my head: I would perform with two instruments. One would be tuned normally. The other would remain in a G tuning. So be it. I would do without the clothes.

I pulled the duffel bag to the floor right there in the middle of the terminal. A confusion of clothes and personal effects was strewn all over just to the side of the line of festively dressed people on their way to the same flight. Everyone looked down at me and those Israeli machine guns and no doubt breathed a sigh of relief that the nice man with the .44 revolver on his hip was making the airways safe for vacation travel. Bob was pretending not to be there at all. I dug through jeans, jewelry, jackets, belts, shirts, socks, and shoes. I chose a pair of gym shorts, a couple of T-shirts, some socks, and a pair of sandals. I quickly stuffed them in the small black bag. It now looked rather pregnant, but it worked.

The last I saw of poor old Bob, he was on the escalator with the big duffel bag full of clothes and machine-gun parts.

The security cop passed me and my guitars through the safety check. I boarded the plane for Miami with the expectant black bag under my arm. By the time I reached Florida, I had written parts of two songs.

♪ *XXVII* ♪

Adrift in Paradise

Sarah,

What a charactered, beautiful, and old Caribbean town, Frederiksted. I'm going to draw some here to show you. The chart houses, story after haphazard story up and down the hills. Wonderfully gabled, louvered, archways in stone, heavy storm windows of wood fastened and latched, pinks and tangerines, and pastels of blue, courtyards, stone and stuccoed walls narrow the lanes to where the Antiguian and I can't help but salute each other as we pass.

Got three loaves of the local bread. Heavy and warm. Three bucks. Kate is my landlady. She's getting me a white cheese from the market. She loves to smile.

Vince

I disembarked on St. Croix on one of those rollaway staircases. The air was heavy with water. Steamy warm. As I entered the two-room terminal without air conditioning, the collar on my shirt instantly relaxed to my shoulders. Mike Walters and I shook hands and fetched my guitar cases from the outdoor baggage pickup. No baggage check, and no one asked for my baggage stubs. I could get used to this.

In fewer than ten minutes we drove from the coast up a short hill to where his big house stood with its louvered bay windows. Next to it was a large windmill that groaned and squeaked when the wind blew, and the wind always blew. What a background noise that was to the songs I wrote.

Mike's neighborhood was a collection of copiously overgrown and wildly flowering, mostly undeveloped lots overlooking the Caribbean side of St. Croix a mile or so from Frederiksted. Flowers were every-where—on trees, in huge bushes, along the road, between houses, and crowding vacant lots.

The phone at Mike's was on an old party line. We shared the line with Kate's house. She would shout from her porch if the caller wanted to speak with one of us. She kidded me constantly about my long-distance affair with Sarah and affably helped me feel good about myself, even when my stay got tenuous. It tried to, almost from the outset.

That first night, I was scheduled to perform at the Hurricane Bar in Christiansted. I changed into one of my clean T-shirts and threw both guitars into the back of Mike's pickup. The bar was open-air with a cooling breeze throughout. There were world-class sailboats in the tiny harbor and brightly colored villas lining the shore in both directions.

"Vince Bell?" said a man my age.

"You got'm." I smiled, shook his hand, and he introduced himself as the fellow musician, David, who had booked me into the gigs.

With a sigh he began, "I love the tape you sent. It was easy to book you because of it. But listen, this squirrel-bait club manager here has been pissing people off all over the island lately. My band and I won't work for him any longer, and we're the most popular in town. We don't trust him. But it wasn't that way when I booked you last month. I hope nothing goes wrong." He was genuinely caring and worried.

A small, unassuming fellow with a mustache found me gawking at a sunbather on an adjoining verandah. "They don't make them like that in Texas, do they?" he opened casually but with a businesslike tone. So this was the manager.

"I'm living on the coast in California these days and yes, it looks rather like that," I parried.

"Vince, good to have you on-island. How do you like it so far?"

"It's an eyeful. So, where do you want me to put these guitars?"

"Uh, that's going to be a problem tonight. Hurricane Hugo ran through here and tore up this island last year. We haven't had the business we used to. What I'd really appreciate you doing is let us cancel on you tonight. I mean, you're here for a while, aren't you?"

"Yes," the shoe hit the floor.

"Let's scrub tonight, 'cause no one is going to be here. We'll start you tomorrow for an afternoon show at two o'clock. We have a built-in crowd of locals that show up on Sunday afternoon."

"You know your business, pal, whatever you say." I still had most of five weeks of dates at more clubs in this little Dutch town. It never was my style to make waves unnecessarily. The phone rang and the manager excused himself.

While Mike and David were consoling me over a beer, I ordered another round, this time dark Amstels. When the waitress brought those tall bottles, I told her I was playing during the next weeks. The club would pick up the tab. She informed me dryly, "Sorry, that'll be $2.50 apiece. Entertainers don't drink free at the Hurricane Bar."

I could hear the other shoe drop like a stone.

The next day, I got there early and set up my instruments. I played for two hours of my three-hour gig before the manager called me aside to pay me off for half the date. I guessed he didn't like my songs. He said they wouldn't be needing me any longer. "It's just business, you know?"

It was shocking to have traveled that far and have things go that badly right off the bat. I hadn't been shorted money for a gig, much less a series of dates over a month, in 20 years.

The ride back to Mike's was very quiet. But when we got there, we polished off a full bottle of coconut liqueur and Coke out on the deck as the sun went down. We chuckled hard while laying into that weasel of a club manager. David called to express his angst. I agreed how unfortunate it was but repeated my thanks for trying to help me out and told him not to worry about it. "I've been dead for almost a decade now." The cool breeze off the Caribbean was steady through the house as we bedded down for the night.

About midnight, I awoke and began a ritual I would follow for the duration of my stay on that picturesque but lonely little island. I dialed up Sarah, five time zones away. She answered with a cheerful "Hello?" about seven o'clock her time. She had just come home from a day in downtown Berkeley fundraising for nonprofits like Greenpeace and the Sierra Club. I said, "Some midget with a mustache and trash can lids for ears canceled me for half a dozen dates today."

She said, "Don't worry, Vince, you're the best. Hang in there; you've got a long way to go."

"But I've got to pay Fitz back for the $500 plane ticket. This puts a serious kink in those plans."

"Maybe you should tell him that you can't, or that you will pay him back as much as you can. It's not your fault . . ."

Then the remote phone went dead, and the pretty girl I was talking to a soothing moment before was gone, gone, gone. Days later, I would learn from trial and error that it took an hour and a half to recharge the remote sufficiently to make another long distance call.

> Sarah,
>   Talking to you in these letters is one of the most important things I do. I've cried at you, bitched at you, recited to you, whimpered at you, composed at you, flailed at you, trailed after you, lost you, left you, missed you, given up on you, forgotten you, thought of you, cared for you for years. I don't want to be easy to get rid of anymore.
>   Vince

That girl was as good to me as Bob was. I loved her for being so supportive of me, no matter how far away I was. I decided that the best thing for me was to keep moving, keep brainstorming ways to succeed, no matter the price. I dreamed that night as I lay in the sea breeze that I was as good as she said. By the next day, the indignity of yesterday was just that, impossible for a head-injured dude to remember.

At the end of the first week, my next gig was at the Wreck Bar. It was a night club owned by Texans, I was told. I assumed that information was for my benefit.

To get to town, I would walk the better part of a mile from Mike's to Centerline Road. When a taxi driver saw me standing by the side of the road, he pulled over and charged me the requisite few American dollars to ride wherever I wanted to go to along Centerline up to as far as the clock steeple in town.

I arrived in Christiansted just before dark. I lugged my effects the remaining few hundred yards to the ramshackle bar on Hospital Street. Looking down to check the time, I saw that the watch I had worn since the mental institution was gone. The unthinkable had occurred. I had lost my watch in that taxi.

I was very disappointed in myself. I scolded, "Head-injured people don't recall enough to lose the precious few things that mean anything to them, pal." I grieved for days about that little companion of mine, the watch.

With a gig imminent, my nerves were twitching to the fingertips in my errant arms. It was such a challenge to perform someplace new and, in the harsh light of the Hurricane Bar's cancellations, performing anyplace at all.

The Wreck Bar didn't look open—or like a bar, for that matter. Far in the back of the littered lot, behind an arched stone wall that was falling down around a few partially varnished picnic tables, was a dirty-looking little service bar with some faded beer advertisements stapled to it. I made my way through the picnic tables and put my guitar down in front of the bar. As I leaned on the well-worn, weathered mahogany the bartender stuck out his hand, saying, "I hear you been to the Hurricane Bar?"

"Yeah, I don't think I'll be seeing them again."

When the night was over, I had played three hour-long sets to some pretty bored people underneath a yellow bug light hung three feet from my head. They stayed, nonetheless, sitting on whatever they could find in that reliquary of telephone wire spools and rusting boatyard flotsam. I was half-drunk from the Texas beer the bartender kept sending me. After I put the PA back in the sailor shack, I gratefully took the money and the next date they offered.

After a half dozen other cancellations at bars all over Christiansted, things looked grim for the home team. I changed my mind about not playing happy-hour and afternoon or lunchtime performances. I would do anything that would make the money to pay Fitz back for that plane ticket. Mostly I did extra gigs they gave me at the Wreck Bar, but I also played midtown under the steeple. I'd just take the guitar out of the case and start singing away to tourists. Some tipped me, some didn't even notice me. I liked the shaded spots the best.

One evening, after a paying gig at the Wreck Bar, I sat for an extra hour beside the bar telling lies and war stories with some of the locals. Before long I was feeling no pain, after a half dozen of those Texas beers. I weaved along Hospital Street to the steeple where I had parked Mike's pickup. With the guitar and the black bag in the bed behind the cab, I proceeded up Queen Street looking for a turnoff to the road across the island. There are very few street signs in paradise.

The car following me began to reflect in the red of my taillights just as his flashing, bright lights filled my rearview mirror. I stopped the car,

fished my wallet from my pocket, and got out. Two Christiansted policemen met me, smiling. They were in typically good humor as they took
my stateside license. They eyed me up and down for a moment. One
said, "Do you know you were going down this lane the wrong way?"

"No sir." They asked me to "walk the line." I said, "I'm head-injured,
fellas, and I couldn't walk a straight line if I was stone-cold sober. I've
been playing at the Wreck Bar half the night."

They returned in British accents, "We think you've been drinking,
Mr. Bell."

I said diffidently, "Bullet proof and invisible."

They practically hit the cobbles in that lane, laughing. "Now, we
can't let you go, Mr. Bell, because you're drunk. But if you'll agree,
we'll take you to the station and let you sleep it off in one of the of-
fices. You won't even have to be in jail. All right, Mr. Bell?"

I couldn't believe my ears. Caught behind the wheel of a moving
vehicle, sheets to the wind, and these fellows were just going to let me
sleep it off in someone's office? I had to promise never to drive drunk
on the island again, but at that moment I wanted to live in the Virgins
the rest of my life.

A promise is a promise. The next night I took a taxi to the gig. I knew I
would be drinking that Texas beer, and I didn't want there to be a chance
in hell that I would repeat last night's performance. With the gig completed and the money in hand, I weaved to the block by that steeple clock.
I waited for what seemed like forever to take the taxi back across island.
After a while I lay down on my guitar case. Tourists and their dates walked
around me. I fell asleep. I was awakened under the gleam of an automobile
bumper by an eight-cylinder engine purring over my head. It was one of
the same policemen. He said, rather incredulously, "What are you doing?"

"I'm waiting for a taxi. I told you guys I wouldn't drive drunk, and
I'm not."

He explained, "The taxi won't be back here until seven o'clock in the morning. You're too late. It stopped running about 11:30. Come on, get in the back of the car. I'm taking you to the station."

Twice in two nights? Probably wasn't even a record.

A few evenings later I was under that bug light at the Wreck Bar. After I finished a popular song by some English group, I looked down around the side of the stage. There stood those two policemen, smiling widely. "We just stopped by to see if you were OK."

For the five weeks I was in the Virgin Islands, I called Sarah several times every evening. I would call after a gig past midnight my time and talk for 18 minutes, put the phone back in its cradle for a couple of hours, then call back. On Sundays we would do this all afternoon and into the evenings.

Mike left for the States and I was now carless and 15 miles from the gigs I had left. A bigger problem was my lack of money, and it became necessary to financially batten down. For the last half of my stay in the Virgins, my meals consisted of one loaf of the local bread per day from the National Bakery in Frederiksted. The bakery was a little, unadvertised, open-air storefront business that I had discovered on my wanderings. It would open for about an hour the morning of bread-making day until they would sell out, close, and go fishing. No one there spoke English nor did any business with the American population on the island. We used a word or two of Spanish with sign language to communicate numbers of loaves and, most important, dollars in return. I liked them. They smiled at me every week.

> Sarah,
>   Almost a month later of letters every day. Can you take this anymore? If you said "yes," then please press the blue button. You will be dispensed 3 coffee-flavored pills to keep you lucid through the next two weeks of more letters.
>   If you said "no," then please press the yellow button. You

will be dispensed 3 coffee-flavored pills to keep you lucid through the next two weeks of more letters.

If you said "none of the above," you will be given another pencil.

Vince

The next day the phone rang. I picked it up after Kate yelled from the screened-in porch of her house a hundred feet away, "It's for you, Vince."

"Hello? Oh hello, Fitz, good to hear from you. Howz Mike?" This was my first communication with the man that had fronted me a half a thousand dollars for the plane ticket to come here almost five weeks ago. "So, when am I going to get to meet you? Dinner at your place sounds great. No, the directions to your house are here on the counter. Mike left them in case I needed anyone . . . I sure will, and thanks again for the invitation. I look forward to meeting you and your wife."

On the following day, I taxied and walked to a small town way north of Centerline and found the country-lane address. I met the statuesque and handsome, bronze-skinned man in the gravel drive next to an immaculate lawn. He was impressive in size and build. He shook my hand solidly as we walked together to the side door of the one-story, bay-windowed house. His wife smilingly introduced herself, setting a tray of finger sandwiches between us in a comfortably appointed den off the dining room.

Fitz explained his West Indian background briefly in a commanding yet cordially deep voice. He was from a small town on St. Martin, down the archipelago of islands that ran toward the equator to South America. With a daughter in college in New York City and the water business with Mike on several of the islands, he had had no time to see me play this trip, he said apologetically. But he hoped that would change if I came back.

Not once in my pleasant visit was the subject of my indebtedness to him mentioned. I left determined to pay that man and his lovely wife back every cent he had the confidence to loan me, sight unseen.

> Sarah,
>> Fitz asked me with a straight face over dinner whether I thought I was a better guitar player than he. I told him I'd wager. He laughed.
>> Vince

I had squirreled away a hundred dollars a week by eating nothing but those loaves sold by the pretty Creole girls behind the counter at the bakery. They always saved me a couple of fresh ones, even when I was late getting there on foot. It was now down to the wire if I was going to be able to pay Fitz back in full. So many things had gone wrong. So many dates had been canceled. But I was still in the ball park. I recalled having written, "Your gift is that you are relentless."

The next evening I was in the square by the steeple playing yet another Eagles song when the bartender of the Wreck Bar stopped with a case of beer on his shoulder. Hefting it with one strong arm to his thigh, he said, "Come play for tips anytime you want. You're bound to be able to make more there than in front of this damned church." With only a couple of days left before I returned to California, I agreed. And I was only short $50 now.

> Sarah,
>> I'd be so lonely without you to talk to with this pen. I guess that's the downside of being on a tropical island with a house all to yourself. There are four beds for someone who could never fall asleep in more than a half of one anyway.
>> The object now seems to be to get off this island, after two nights in the cop stop, six new songs, eight cancellations, and 13 gigs in 37 days and nights on the equator.
>> Vince

The afternoon before I departed, I earned $30 in tips playing from lunch to damn near dinnertime in that now homelike confusion of the Wreck Bar. Exhausted, I wanted to change my coins and one-dollar bills for tens like the stack of them I had back at Mike's. The bartender sifted through the collection of small change, hardly counting. "So," he asked, "how much you short?"

"Twenty bucks."

He cranked the handle, *ding-DING*, reached into the ancient register that didn't even display the right amounts, and pulled out a crisp twenty. "Here . . . you deserve it. Been good to know you."

QUEEN STREET

First light and he draws the shades,
surrey pulling down the lane.
Clip, clop, clip, clopping cobbles
echo 'cross the alleyway.
The pastor strolls 'neath arches,
orchids overgrow window boxes.
Tick, tock, tick, tocking clockworks
in the steeple as it rains.

Cream-colored walls, a creaking fan,
table settings for no one.
Photos scattered about an ashtray,
a little dog, a gentle hand.
Granite floors and window stalls,
daybreak plays upon a painting.
And though the strokes are like Gaugin,
the sands are by a different . . . ocean.

The bird alights the flower tree,
and caws a caw that calls to him.
Curving neck and graceful beak
yet, as she speaks,
she's gone again.
Shadows move, but nothing changes,
like the painting of the sea.
Sunlight shallows into the depths,
at 33 Queen Street.

♪ *XXVIII* ♪

Give Chance a Chance

Sarah,

My memories of the West Indies are fresh and nostalgic. I think I'll always believe it was a charmed time, even through all the cancellations. One of the best parts was talking to you.

I remember the flower tree full of birds next to a green sea with no waves. I'll never forget negotiating the price of bread in those Caribbean towns, and drinking the local rum.

Two days gone from the islands and my memories glow, but not as brightly as my thoughts of you.

Vince

*B*ob Sturtevant remembers, "The time in the Virgin Islands was not easy for Vince, but I felt it would be good for him to go out there and get stretched. Of course, I didn't know that he was going to have nothing to eat but bread for a month. But when he came back, he had had an adventure, and I think he felt more independent. And he did make enough money to pay Fitz back, which is Vince from A to Z—he settles his accounts."

Sarah,

Seeing you was the best. We've been apart for years. It's like no time has elapsed. This last weekend was magic. I don't feel like a victim anymore. I wanna be a star in your movie.

Vince

More long-distance phone calls and two weeks later, I packed up my belongings for the drive to San Francisco. I was moving.

My first few weeks were spent at a good friend's, Hobart Taylor. Hobart and I had met in Houston over 15 years ago. We had had many friends in common over those years, which helped us conceive a new business relationship. Hobart became my manager, and with the tact of a statesman, he announced my renaissance into music.

"I was living in San Francisco when Vince had his accident," says Hobart, "and working with Lucinda Williams at the time. I came to Texas once or twice a year, and Vince and I would visit for an hour or two, or a lunch. Because I didn't see him regularly, I could watch the changes like snapshots. In the early days, he was definitely tentative, a wounded puppy. I was convinced from the first, because of his arrogance and strength, that he'd whip it.

"A couple of the earliest memories I have of Vince are of how much he loved dogs, and the incredible relationship he had with them. Another is one of the first times I met Vince before the accident. It was upstairs in the backroom at Houlihan's in Houston. He was really full of himself, energetic and powerful. The impression I had was that this was someone who definitely thought he was a legend in his own time. Of course then I got to know and love him.

"A major difference after the accident was that he really focused on you and what you said rather than talking about himself all the time.

"I had always wanted to work with Vince. I had told a friend years before that Vince was one of the great songwriters in Houston, that he was also a great performer and had star quality. I was a little intimidated by him and wanted to work with Lucinda for a while and see how that went before I approached Vince about working together. When he came to San Francisco, I was really happy to see him, and glad I had a situation that let him live with me for a while. I really loved him. I didn't know quite what we were going to do, but I thought he had written some of the best songs ever and that it would be great to get them known—to show them to some of the people I had been meeting, if nothing else. He convinced me to be his manager. His wry wit and strong sense of irony also convinced me that he still had it.

"It wasn't easy, though. When you start managing someone you always see the optimal outcome, but the experience is often different. You have to go on and hope that some of the world will see what you are trying to do and be ever-so-slowly influenced. There were three things I thought that Vince needed to do at that point, after being away from the business for so long: He needed to perform, he needed the experience of recording, and, although he was writing, he needed the time and space to write more. He did perform some. It was rough, but it was fun to watch him work his magic. It was good for him to get the feedback on new songs that live performance gives."

A short while later, I left Hobart's, and slowly Sarah and I absorbed my guitars, cafe table, and a trash can bottom covered in pennies into a small apartment she had in the Oakland Hills.

When I left for the islands, the dark-topped Martin that had been involuntarily wrested from my grasp became my main squeeze again. The day shortly followed when I put down my sister's guitar for good. Her guitar and the little keyboard back in Texas had helped me get my strength back, and for that I will be eternally grateful. Now I strung my old friend up with a set of extra-light strings.

I used the cheapest bronze strings known to man. I bought them from a little out-of-the-way shop in Berkeley that specialized in used musical equipment. There were walls of the ancient Silvertones, Gibsons, Martins, Dan Electros, Harmonys, Nationals, Vegas, and a fair smattering of knockoff models from Japan. The strings hung straight, in tubes marked by their size. There was a tube for .054s, a tube for .042s, and so on, and you made up your own sets. When you finished, you would wrap the six around one another and stuff them in one of the old guitar-string plastics you had saved. They cost $1.75 a set that way. Goodness knows what kind they were. Only goodness cares, when you change them as often as I did. Sometimes every night, depending on how hard I had played.

Sarah says, "I was living a very nine-to-five life, and you immediately went to work, too. You were running a mile or two every day, and you rehearsed endlessly. We went to the Y, and walked a lot, and those walks were never 'Let's get out and wander around in the fresh air.' You were 'bookin',' as you called it. You were very worried about your stomach muscles and working on those, relaxing them so you could walk more naturally.

"You also began recording your songs, trying to relearn and rearrange them, and to get comfortable with them. You really didn't seem comfortable with your songs yet, neither playing them nor singing them, and you certainly didn't seem comfortable performing."

My first San Francisco date was at a club near the Mission District called the Paradise. My night in paradise was shared with a women's rock 'n' roll band. The problem was that the rocket scientists who arranged the shows had the band playing downstairs at the same time I was playing upstairs. An opening in the floor between stages meant that my audience and I got to hear them as loudly as the front row downstairs. For three set's worth that evening, I got a bass guitar enema through the stool I sat on that night. And the entertainment lawyer I invited down to see me was hardly impressed.

It peaced me out for days, and the club never asked me back.

My next gig was for the head-injured. Ever since the accident, I had had a burning commitment to communicate with others of my kind. Berkeley supported a halfway house for survivors of traumatic brain injury. I was heartened to hear this. One of the shortcomings of my own ongoing rehabilitation had been that I was so devastatingly alone without benefit of companionship, or advice, or just plain old conversation. I went to some length to make this concert happen but when I arrived, I found a room full of disinterested people in varying stages of disrepair after their bouts with fate.

I tried to talk to whoever would listen. Big miscalculation. The TV set was the interesting thing in that room. No one had told that disparate group about my arrival. When an employee finally barked instructions to order the room for my performance, turned the set off, and introduced me, I had been sitting there, with my guitar in my lap, through most of a popular half-hour sitcom. One younger fellow got the nerve to ask, "Are you famous?" The syllables slurring.

I looked right into him with all the compassion I could muster, "No, I'm Vince. Who are you?"

He shrunk back into his forced posture and trembled like a boy with nerve damage. I played a few tunes, had a laugh or two with the assembled group, and told them I would come back anytime they wanted. The employee broke back into the room, saying, "OK, it's time for you to go to bed." That was all I needed to hear. It was as tough here for us head-injured as it was any place else on this misunderstanding and impatient planet.

The hardest truth to the whole misbegotten exercise was that I had thought I could go in with my palms up and offer my best to people who deserved the best; but who the hell did I think I was to walk in there bigger than Texas and try to help anyone?

I didn't volunteer again for a decade. When I did, it was for various state conferences for their brain injury associations. In Texas, New Jersey, and Wisconsin I made the early morning keynote address, telling my story and playing a couple of songs, to huge rooms crowded with medical staff and therapists, advocates, survivors, mothers, and even politicians. In the afternoon, I would sit in breakout sessions for survivors and caregivers, play guitar, and answer questions. These, too, were usually well-attended, though the session across the hall with the title "Intimacy after Brain Injury" stole a few of my audience in Wisconsin.

I was to learn another hard truth: that there was a price to pay. I never felt more brain injured than I did when trying to help someone else who was brain injured.

About this time, I lucked into another music twist: I reinvented my pick style. It was a huge adaptation and resulted in a flood of ability. The new pick style was inspired by, and resembled, frailing on a banjo. It would revolutionize my music. While trying to write the song "Girl Who Never Saw a Mountain," I came upon a strum with the thumb and middle finger. And it was smooth. Better yet, with that simple two-pick strum, I discovered I could upstroke with the first finger on the "and" of the beat in the same motion. Backbeat time, folks.

The two-finger strum metamorphosed into a three-finger pick that down-stroked as well, enabling faster tempos and turning the corner on musical phrases of all kinds like a hotrod. My down-stroking with fingerpicks never failed to be noticed—someone was always remarking on my guitar style even if they didn't particularly like what I had to say.

When I changed over from the Travis pick that most people play to my new style of fingerpicking, I was introduced to a new world of capability. I could up-stroke and down-stroke chords, notes, or harmonies across a broad spectrum of sound from the low end to the high. I could choose notes from chord forms in several ways and could mute the strings by palming with my right hand, or add notes by using different chord positions. It was very intuitive when I was playing on the fly, and it was done very much by ear. It was right if it sounded right. Some of the pick styles I dreamed up and began to use would take years to really absorb. The effects they created were worth the effort and the patience—neither of which would have mattered without a healthy disregard for the facts of my condition in those days. Music'll do that to you.

I began recording my tunes with my new pick style while keeping "The Hotel" out of the hands of the law in the East Bay and in a legal parking space somewhere. It was almost November 1990, and the police had begun to leave chalk marks on the tires of the Hotel. The neighbors had apparently had enough of my strange-looking van parked in their neighborhood. In less than two weeks, I sold the good old Hotel to a construction contractor from . . . the West Indies. His accent was British, we knew some of the same islands, and he thought the run-down-looking van would be a good storage place for his tools because thieves would pass it by. OK, so it needed some paint. I sold the 15-year-old Hotel for $500 off the streets of that hoity-toity town. What a hoot.

I began the new year by meeting with music lawyers, seeing other friends play dates, rehearsing accompanists, walking for miles each day in the Oakland Hills, and doing my never-ending vocal exercises. The lawyers came with the impending release of Nanci Griffith's cover of "Sun & Moon & Stars" and Hobart's desire to get some management papers on me. These were expensive conversations, but I had worked for over a decade to have to pay this kind of bill, and I was glad.

In Berkeley, I played at Larry Blake's, an old blues club that was trying out a new format of hiring acoustic-playing writers. I took the bait and gave it my best shot one early evening on Telegraph Avenue. I never heard from them further. Then I played at San Geronimo Civic Center up in Marin County. Again the response was exceptional, I thought, for a one-night stand.

A string of dates followed in Berkeley at Freight and Salvage; in San Francisco at the Ace Cafe, Mondo Java, and the Hotel Utah; and in Davis, California, at the university there. I also played at the Noe

Valley Ministry in San Francisco with Victoria Williams and Michelle Shocked, and up the coast near Mendocino at the Inn in the tiny community of Caspar.

> From a letter to my father:
> I played in San Francisco last night and made seven dollars. Sarah said I sounded pretty good, though. Must have been the guitar. I did my songs at a place called Sacred Ground. Windy name for a beer-and-wine place that serves cookies and sandwiches. It's run by a crusty little old man at a corner just off the Panhandle to Golden Gate Park. It seats maybe 20 people, and last night the seats were largely taken. Anyway, thanks in no small part to the guitar,
> they liked my stuff.

My first trip back to Texas to play was in August '91, about a year and a half after I had moved to California. I played for Craig Hillis in Austin at his club, Saxon Pub, and for Tim Leatherwood in Houston at Anderson Fair. After those dates, I ended up outside of Luling at the Riverbottom Festival, hosted by my Texas friend and lawyer Bill McNeal.

My sister Shary says, "Vince was doing so much better after his move to California. He'd gotten so stagnated and down in Texas. He'd been trying so hard, and he was making progress, but the last couple of years in Texas really dragged him down. He'd lost himself and his sense of humor. When he finally got away, he did nothing but rise. The change has been a joy."

My sister Lana adds, "He was no longer a different person. It had been a slow, rolling process. Now he is as he was."

Back in California, Sarah and I drove down Highway One on the coast south of San Francisco. Our conversation turned from guitars and dramatically beautiful scenery to ourselves for a change. "I don't know, what do you think?" I asked.

"I think we'll be in Half Moon Bay in ten miles."

"No, I mean about getting married." The wind stiffened and we leaned together, our heads on each other's shoulders.

"I think I'd be happy to be married to you, Vince."

'Nuff said.

We stopped at a small seaside restaurant in one of those tiny harbors full of the local fishing boats. Out of the now cold wind, we were seated at a large bay window that looked out into the harbor on the gray and windy sea.

". . . I think my mother will be very happy for me."

"You do?"

"Of course."

Bob Sturtevant says, "For having some feedback, not only in his music but in his life, as to who he is and feeling comfortable, Vince has Sarah to thank. Had he not been able to develop and grow in his personal life, I really don't know what would have happened. I know that she has provided a life for him that he never had. And he needs her.

"I see a security in him and a peace of mind that hadn't been there before, not even before the wreck. A loving relationship eludes so many people, and it has done him so much good to be able to rest. Not that the rehabilitation work doesn't continue to go on, but he seems so much calmer now.

"I think that his songs have taken on a more mature tone. His observations are those that speak of a man older than the man who wrote 'Sun & Moon & Stars,' which was written by someone who was already older than his time then.

"Because I know how deeply the accident injured him, and I've seen him so often, it's remarkable to see how far he's had to come to be able to enjoy his life again."

♪ XXIX ♪

Prize for Not Working Hard Enough

An important project of my Bay Area years was about to begin. There I was, fancying myself some kind of romantic, but I didn't even have my work collected in a place that I could turn to and find the material I boasted about.

Hobart Taylor recalls, "I talked to Townes [Van Zandt] on a trip to Nashville. He thought Vince's work was so good that it should be catalogued. His exact words were, 'Vince is a poet. He should do a songbook.'"

So while we played nine-ball in a China Basin bar on a rainy weekday afternoon, Hobart and I decided to rent some studio space and record the materials I had authored. When the rain stopped, we drove over Portrero Hill back into the city. "That was the most important work we did together—recording about 60 songs over five or six months time," Hobart continued. "The act of recording them means they take a shape, no matter how that might change later. They have an interpretation. It could perhaps make a recording possible."

At the same time, Sarah and I began to type the words to the years of songs I had been writing since the early '70s. The "filing system" we were replacing consisted of typed sheets, Black Book entries, freehand scrawlings on lined and unlined pages, all in a covey of books, backed and unbacked, loose-leaved and spiraled, and all those tunes heretofore on the backs of matchbook covers and bar napkins. The 100 or so songs we came up with we called the *Complete Works of Vince Bell*. Two shorter volumes, the *Selected Works* and the *Recent Works*, had smaller selections of songs. I thought it was the nicest thing I could do for people who were inundated with masses of material. When we finished, I could scroll on that personal computer past every song I had attempted since 1971.

The recording part of the project was done in San Francisco, at Lowdown Studio, run by Greg Freeman. He was a crackerjack engineer who had put the best, if not the prettiest, studio together in the warehouse district of San Francisco. I would take up on a low stool that Greg set up for me under a couple of microphones on boom stands. One for my voice, the other for my guitar. He would adjust the EQs and the volumes and then address me through the headphones: "OK, Vince, you ready?" I would shake the cobwebs from my head and begin. I put down song after song until I was virtually goggle-eyed from recollecting forgotten melodies paired to lyrics.

On a good day I could do fair renditions of upwards of ten songs. In a month of weekly sessions, I completed 59 songs.

Sarah and I sent these tomes of travail with accompanying cassettes to anyone who would listen: record producers, publishers, poets, producers, artists, booking agents, managers, lawyers, and interested friends. They had an introduction that read:

IN 1992 SARAH AND I DESIGNED, PRODUCED,
PACKAGED, AND MAILED APPROXIMATELY 125
SELECTED, COMPLETE, AND RECENT WORKS
COVERING A 20-YEAR AUTHORSHIP IN LYRICS AND
POETRY MADE WITH DOUBLE-SIDED TITLE, INDEX,

AND CHRONOLOGY PAGES SHEATHED IN PLASTIC,
AND I RECORDED 59 TUNES ON MORE THAN 300
HOURS OF CASSETTE TAPE FOR OVER 6,000 PAGES OF
SONG . . . WITH 20,000 HOLE PUNCHES.

One *Selected Works* copy went with a letter that read:

> The trick is to use the conventions in your work to create
> an interpretation like no other. That's art. The anticipated re-
> sult is we musicians won't sound so much alike. Instead, we'll
> have a lot in common.
> Enjoy these 59 Vince tunes on paper and tape. Title index,
> first line index, chronology. There's a lot there, so I don't need
> to tell you to take it a bit at a time. It took me 20 years, and
> from edge to edge in Texas, and it'll take you a few Saturday
> afternoons as well. And it represents my current work, or at
> least the work I will perform these days with
>   my old Martin guitar.

Sarah and I were married on the north side of Lake Tahoe on February 29, 1992—Leap Day, the second most popular day (after Hal-
loween) to be married—with a small band of friends: Bob Sturtevant,
Hobart Taylor, David Rodriguez, Bianca Ellis, and my sister Shary.

That spring I went to see Lyle Lovett in concert at the Berkeley cam-
pus of the University of California. He performed one of my songs,
"I've Had Enough," which he would record in 1998 on his *Step Inside
This House* CD.

I'VE HAD ENOUGH

I've had enough of words and games.
I don't think I know you,
I can't forget your name.
Your eyes are clear,
the way is strange.

The light's in the hallway
if you forget your way.

You were here to be only
what you wanted anyway.
You were sad to be sorry,
you were sorry everyday.
You were here to be loved,
but love's tricked away
from your eyes.

I tell myself I'm least of all to blame,
For these words of my choosing,
for my rules that make the game.
But, my eyes are clear,
I can see the way is strange,
Through the dark of the hallway
that echoes back your name.

I was here to be only
what I wanted anyway.
I was sad to be sorry,
I was sorry every day.
I was here to be loved,
but loves tricked away
from my eyes.

♪ **XXX** ♪

Phoenix

"**A**fter the *Complete Works* was done, I began to think a recording would in fact be possible," says Hobart. "I had a short list of producers in mind, with an eye to sensitivity to music and sensitivity to the artist. Sometimes you'll trade one for the strength of the other, but that's what I had in mind. Todd Rundgren, Van Dyke Parks, Jim Rooney, Elliot Mazer, and T. Bone Burnett were a few. I was listening to T. Bone's latest album and realized that the songs I thought were the best were coproduced by Bob Neuwirth, and that turned my focus to Bob. I'd met him once or twice in Los Angeles with Peter Case and that 'L.A. Folk School,' as I call it—Case, Soles, Steve Young. I was very glad Bob decided to do the project. I was glad, too, that Vince wasn't lumped in with Nashville or something else recognizable. Vince is an individual before a style. Vince's songs are not folk songs, they are art songs. And they are closer to Jacques Brel than Woody Guthrie."

Bob Neuwirth came to the Bay Area to record two songs he had chosen from my *Complete Works*. He chose "Frankenstein," written by Gary Burgess, a young Houston writer and a friend of mine, performed at half the tempo I had ever done it, and "Girl Who Never Saw a Mountain." Upon the completion of these two cuts with Geoff Muldaur and Fritz Richmond, he decided to take on the rest of the album.

Geoff, like Bob, was masterful working with musical interpretation. He was a favorite of mine from the outset. During that first session, he put his banjo down in the middle of a cut with Fritz Richmond on washtub bass. Noticing my downstroke with fingerpicks, he said, to no one in particular, "Look at how he's playing the guitar." He endeared himself to me for noticing what my dogged work had produced. He took me aside and asked with a smile, "Is this your first album?"

"Yes," I said.

"Good, get it over with."

We had recorded those in November. December that year was the tenth after my wreck. I played New Year's in San Francisco at a washateria that served beer.

The year 1993 opened with the greatest expectations of my musical career. The two songs I had completed with Bob Neuwirth, Geoff, and Fritz kept my spirits stratospheric as I hoofed it day after day through the Berkeley hills. The funny thing about my progress now was that it was invisible even to me, more often than not, though on occasion I was faced with grim reminders. Those were some of my worst moments. The quandary of memory, the clubfootedness and my balance, the aches in my arm, or the self-doubt in my heart would sometimes leave me sitting on the curb with my head in my hands. The veil still lifted to reveal that the enigmas had gone nowhere. They were only held at bay by tricks.

The fact remained that I could never wake up to a new day and not be head-injured. I could never quite shake the feeling of aloneness that the years of quiet determination had left. My efforts to retrieve myself from an anonymous life devoid of any quality had left me convinced that I had precious little in common with anyone else. The harder I jabbed, the longer I struggled, the deeper I dove into an enigmatic state where the consequences remained fearful and unclear. I tried not to be overtaken by the ghosts just behind my mind's eye.

Music rehearsal now intensified. The daily routines of scales and endless chord structures to strengthen my rebuilt right arm and dyslexic left arm progressed. Guitar and vocal exercises continued as I worked on new arrangements for the songs for my recording. In some cases I rearranged songs that I had never performed. My material was being called out onto the mat.

Fifty bucks bought an airline-shuttle ticket from Oakland to Burbank in Southern California. In a booth in a restaurant on Lincoln Boulevard, Bob Neuwirth said, as he was leafing through his copy of the *Complete Works*, "What's this?" He pointed to a song called "Hard Road."

"That's a pretty good little country song I wrote in Tahoe back in the '70s." I didn't let on, but it was one of those I had never performed before.

"Let's do it," he said.

I accepted the challenge.

Choosing some of the songs for my album in such an intuitive fashion minus any musical renditions gave me an indescribable confidence in all the materials I had labored over. According to the producer, I hadn't wasted the last two decades. It made me feel like the circuitous crawl back from the wreck was worth it. "DAMAGED BOY REINVENTS MUSIC." There was a reason for the dauntingly large *Complete Works*. I had "ten years' worth of recordings in it," Bob told me.

It was a rocking two weeks at the end of February. We closed out the arrangements for two or three more pieces. The warm-up song for those sessions was the old war dog that I had campaigned for so many years, "Sun & Moon & Stars." It turned out to be the cut we used on the album. My old fiddle-playing buddy from Nashville, Jim

Justice, and the Bay Area fretless bass player, Paul Logan, teamed with me to make the unanticipated magic happen.

Ten days later, Bob came back to mix the sessions with the crack engineers we used, Tom Doty and Mike Underwood. The occasion allowed me to meet some of Bob's long-time friends, Polly and Charlie Frizzell, who lived in Berkeley also. The first time I listened to a mix of my album would be sitting in their kitchen.

During my recording sessions, Nanci Griffith's second recording of a song of mine, "Woman of the Phoenix," hit the racks in the record stores on her album *Other Voices, Other Rooms.* In March, Sarah and I flew to New York City and I sang a song, along with many others, at Nanci's Carnegie Hall date. On the plane home, I couldn't help the thought that someone with a partially paralyzed vocal cord sang at Carnegie Hall.

In April of that year, I played in San Francisco at the Bottom of the Hill with Peter Case. I later flew to L.A. with Hobart to do some ancillary business with the co-publisher of several of my songs, Bug Music. In Berkeley, Nanci Griffith invited me to see her Zellerbach show from the wings.

I received a phone call from my mother. She was very weak from the cancer treatments she had been enduring. She said, "Vince, I don't feel so well."

I tried to be her support and replied, "Hang in there, Mom. You're sounding better all the time."

"I'm so tired."

"Why don't you try and get some rest. When you wake up, call me again."

Both Sarah and I said good-night to her.

Several hours later, the phone rang again. It was my sister Shary. "Vince, it's about Mom . . ."

"Yeah, I just talked to her. Those treatments seem to have her down, but she sounded better to me than she has in a while . . ."

"Vince, I'm sorry, but Mom has passed away."

I was confused. But she was sounding good, I thought.

My mother died on May 12, 1993.

On my birthday of the previous year, my dear mother had written:

> My Dearest Son,
>   I want to wish you all the best that life has to offer on your 41st birthday—I am so proud of you and the man that you have become—I feel now that I have a strong shoulder to lean on, if it becomes necessary—but most of all, thanks for bringing Sarah into our lives—I love you with all my heart, and hope you have 100+ more birthdays.
> Always,
Your Mother

My album would be dedicated "to my brother, her, and . . . me."

My mother once said to me of an incident that hurt her badly, "I cried my tears." And I did. I could only take heart in the fact that she had heard the pre-mastered versions of those outstanding tapes that Bob Neuwirth was helping me work through. She'd always believed in me and my work and told me I was the best. I had been faithfully sending her the results of every subsequent session to keep her spirits up. It meant everything to me for her to see how well I was doing after how low I had been laid down. I wanted her to be secure that her kid was just fine, that the best she ever was came out in me.

When I returned to the Bay from her funeral, I found that it had been arranged for me to perform in Los Angeles at the Troubadours of Folk Festival in June. The show included such long-time luminaries as Richie Havens, the Jefferson Airplane, and Joni Mitchell. I played the second stage with stalwarts like Richard Thompson and John Hammond, Jr.

That same month, Bob Neuwirth came back to San Francisco and we recorded the rest of my album's basic tracks in that studio in the Tenderloin, Hyde Street Studio. I met more of the crew of the album's contributors, including Bill Rich, a respected bass player of long standing. Bill had played with Jimi Hendrix and had been a member of The Butterfield Blues Band with Geoff Muldaur. Victoria Williams has one of the more expressive voices in music. She had recently been on tour with Neil Young and was now doing wonderful albums of her own. Geoff sat there, expressionless, with a slide in one hand. In the other was a finely aged, sunburst National acoustic guitar with a cutaway and a mother-of-pearl headstock. In two decades of looking, I had never seen an instrument so grand as that.

As we embarked on a song, Bob would gaze atmospherically through the double panes, a hand on his chin, or with arms folded. In a relaxed motion, he reached out and pressed a button on the massive studio console in the control room. Click . . . (Pause). "Vince, you sang that last one just like Caruso." (Pause) . . . click.

"Thanks, Bob." I puffed up like a rookie in front of the distinguished musicians, whose eyes now wandered about the room.

Click . . . (pause). "But Vince" (pause, and now a little more emphatically), "you aren't Caruso. Just tell the story, OK? Try it again." (Pause) . . . click.

In four working days that hot July, we recorded the eight remaining songs, sitting across from each other in a square around the vocal mics as Victoria and I sang our parts. Minus overdubs to come in later from John Cale in New York City, Lyle Lovett in Los Angeles, and Steve Bruton in Austin, my album had been done live and in person. The final overdubs would be put on at Hyde Street Studio by Mickey Raphael and David Mansfield. Around my guitar and voice parts were some of the best players in contemporary music. My rebuilt, re-trained arm and I were at the center.

From a letter to Victoria Williams:

The Cover Charge Is to Get Out
　I've listened to our singing at Hyde Street, often remarking on your vocals and enjoying them greatly. You did a wonderful job. My current favorite is one of several, and never the same one twice in a row.
　You have been one of the biggest supporters of me and my guitar. I will welcome any occasion to sing with you again. It says in the closing lyric to "Mirror, Mirror":

> As you believed in me
> So you shall ever be,
> Fairest of them all.

And so you shall.
vince

Bob Neuwirth showed up at my house one day and referred to the album as *Phoenix*. The name stuck.

Throughout the rest of 1993 I listened to the new overdubs as they came past my desk. I played boring dates in Half Moon Bay, the Mission District over in the city, and Calistoga. The hardest lesson I had learned in the previous 11 years was how to do nothing at all. It came in handy now.

Sarah and I decided to move back to Texas after my master tapes were picked up by an independent record label from, that's right . . . Austin, Texas. Sarah recounts, "We spent the next year trying to get some bookings while Bob Neuwirth was looking for a label. In February 1994, it looked as though he was going to recommend Watermelon Records, and we decided it was time to move back to Texas if your album was going to be on a Texas label."

In February of '94, I played a concert at Anderson Fair in Houston, so the trip and a week's worth of cheap motel room in Central Texas were paid for while we looked for a place to live there. When I took the stage and sang the better part of an hour's worth of material from *Phoenix*, Tim Leatherwood said to Sarah, "Vince has to learn how to sing louder." So much for the progress I thought I had made.

"Vince's progress had been such a slow process that you almost lost track if you weren't the person having to deal with that continual uphill grade," Tim says. "Vince was one of the most immaculate musicians. He was a natural. He's got to be one of the best songwriters I've ever heard. His songs have stood up to all kinds of tests. I was glad he was able to work with Neuwirth, because Bob has the most patience of anybody I know for extracting out of someone what it is that they're trying to do. He's not a quick producer that wants to pump things out. He'll sit on a song until something happens that works right. It was a great match."

Before the week was up, we wrung the unlimited mileage out of a rent car looking for a house in the Texas Hill Country. It finally happened around one corner of a block near Fredericksburg's attractive, old-fashioned downtown. In a large yard full of leafless old pecan and hackberry trees was a yellow-painted, gingerbread-trimmed 1920s house with a limestone front porch with a green porch swing. The paint was peeling on the old place, and inside the walls were dingy, but it was big and sunny. The ceilings were 11 feet high.

The night we arrived in Fredericksburg, Nanci Griffith won a Grammy Award for her *Other Voices, Other Rooms* with my song on it.

WOMAN OF THE PHOENIX

I've listened to the words you lovers speak,
the sounds of the lovers' song.
And I've dreamed
all the dreams that the wayward son dreams
in a thousand places gone.
Dallas was my late night out
and Ratcliff served to roust me out.
Houston lay like Cleveland
with the color removed.

All I ever wanted
was to wander and to woo
a woman of the phoenix,
a welcome Waterloo.

I've seen the sun
blaze the breasts of the countryside.
I've seen her huddled
in a winter freeze.
And I've run 'cross paths
of a thousand lives,
among the cactus and the white birch trees.

Avlock ran a waterfront bar.
Vito he was the king of thieves.
Michael was a rock-and-roll hood
from the Odessa plains.
All of them were my kind,
wild and damned near free,
but a woman of the phoenix
was the medicine for me.

Six weeks later, I attended South by Southwest in Austin. At one of the parties, in the ballroom of the Driskill Hotel, I met Germans, Italians, and English among record-company executives from New

York and Los Angeles and management personnel from Nashville. I was calm, conversational, and no one in the room had any idea of my past as I shook hands and small-talked my way through the evening. I wore a pair of cowboy boots with riding heels and found my way around that crowded room without the hint of a limp.

In the spring I was invited to speak at the annual Texas Brain Injury Association conference in Austin. A former Dallas Cowboy, a lawyer, and I were among others asked to speak at a breakout session for accident and stroke victims so that they could listen and talk to other survivors. They needed to glimpse someone who had crawled and kicked his way back into the world of the able. That's what they got. In a large conference room, I showed up with my guitar. The packed chamber was filled with ill-fated individuals who were just the way I had been once upon a time. Some were in wheelchairs for life. Some used laptop computers to mechanically speak at all. Some gazed out with the same lightheaded expression that I had worn. I could look back into their weary eyes and track every one of their downtrodden thoughts.

With a big smile, I turned out a selection of songs from *Phoenix* as if they were second nature. I did not make a speech, nor tell them what I did to retrieve myself, nor clumsily suggest what they should do. I just tried to show them that if they wanted it as badly as I had, they could have it. Sarah sat in the front row and choked back tears like a champ. I found myself wishing someone like her for every disheveled, rough-looking man or woman, boy or girl, in the bunch. As I closed my third song, I told them that any head-injured person anywhere interested in seeing my shows could come for free. That will never change. I had gone a length to be there that day. I wanted to do more.

I answered questions, signed autographs, and talked about their desperately desirous tomorrows for an hour. There is an entire industry built around people like the unfortunates I played for that day in

Austin. For all its profit and respectability, that industry still couldn't offer me, or my puzzling friends, a glimmer of hope.

Bob Neuwirth had decided the order of songs for *Phoenix,* and the opening cut was "Frankenstein," about the monster in the old black and white film. When I first heard it, I understood the monster better than I ever had and thought he looked a lot like me.

FRANKENSTEIN
by Gary Burgess

I got stitches all over my body.
My feet are too big for my head.
I don't know why they put me here with the living,
I sure wish that I was dead.
My brain is always running and ticking.
My arms and legs tremble to my feet.
I try to walk straight and tall and narrow,
It's just a stagger with a beat.
They call me Frankenstein.
That's not even my name.
Frankenstein . . . I don't know my name.
Frankenstein . . . I don't know who I am.
I don't know what I've done.
I told him, "Victor, you got to build me a woman
who will see me for myself."
It's so lonely living here without someone to love.
I gotta look out for myself.
I seem to scare everyone in the village.
They said I killed someone's little girl.
I remember a child with flowers by the river.
Everything is such a blur.
"I'm an innocent man."

♪ *XXXI* ♪

"Album of a Lifetime"

*P**hoenix* was released on July 16, and the morning began with a radio interview on KUT, the University of Texas's radio station. After lunch with my family, who had come to Austin to help me celebrate the album's release, Geoff Muldaur, David Mansfield, and I had a short rehearsal in the living room of my tiny suite at the old Driskill Hotel.

I had been holding my breath for weeks, hoping I would appear healthy and able to a crowd that would critically watch my every move. Would I panic if I looked out and didn't know where I was? Would I tumble over tricky pronunciations of self-inflicted onomatopoeia? I reminded myself that I was actually pretty good at this stuff now, saying under my breath, "Don't you chickenshit out on me, pal."

At some point during most days, I was lost. My best concepts of time still deserted me, or I would forget what I was doing and why. A few moments of this was more than long enough to leave me unsettled. Then I would pause and get quiet. Doing that often allowed me to catch up to reality, prevented anyone else from noticing my perplexity, and kept me from regarding that condition of my life too seriously. "We had lived together for four years when you told me that sometimes, when you were driving, you had no idea where you were, or where you were going," Sarah recalls.

Early in the afternoon, there was an in-store promotion at Waterloo Records. The event opened with Geoff, David, and me sitting on stools. I was still very self-conscious about standing while I played. The first notes of the show sounded like someone was torturing a small animal, because the guy doing the sound system that day was unsure about how to mic all three of us.

I had to get over my aversion to standing, and fast. In the midst of the next few bars of music, I pulled my right hand away from the pick guard and unplugged the cord from the butt of the Martin in one movement. Without missing a beat, I climbed off of that stool and began to walk slowly out into the audience, performing the piece without micing of any sort. The other two fellows got the giggles and followed along, until we all three stood in the midst of the first few rows of listeners. During the set, I looked around into so many familiar faces. Playing within the crowd of well-wishers was magical.

I finished out the whole set on my feet. "It made him so accessible to people," according to Bob Sturtevant. "When he unplugged the guitar and stood up in the front, that's the Vince I knew, and that was the Vince that everybody was hoping was going to step out, too."

The album release party was later that evening at Cactus Cafe on the University of Texas campus. *Phoenix* got a great send-off that night, though I sat down again when I played. Later, I didn't remember that afternoon when I stood in performance for the first time in 12 years. Some things change hard. Geoff, David, and I comfortably played the songs on the recording to a full house with Bob Neuwirth looking on. I sensed I had made a vast circle somehow complete.

Mandy Mercier describes the night: "Everyone was there—people were there that I hadn't seen since the accident—it was a climactic moment. I didn't know if I'd ever hear Vince sing those old songs again, and now there were new songs and the humor was back. You can't have humor if you have a lot of fear."

"I don't see evidence of head injury when I look at Vince now," comments Hobart. "Perhaps a slight dropout now and again, but that's the same thing you see when you are talking with any really busy, concentrating person who is thinking about several things at the same time, concentrating intensely. I know many musicians who forget more words. His strong desire to work, push, and get as much done as possible probably made all the difference.

"You can take any aspect of a person and mistakenly assume that is the whole person. With Vince you can look for symptoms, but most of the time I just forget. He's too busy being Vince, not a head-injured person. What is essentially him is so strong. The fact that he actually saw the situation for what it was and kept going with dogged tenacity is not only moving, it was inspiring in my own life," Hobart finishes. "The lesson from Vince is that living is in the struggle, and in the work itself. Eventually wider circles will know what we were trying to do: to make people's lives better by providing songs, as Woody Guthrie said, 'that build you up, not tear you down.'"

ROLLING STONE MAGAZINE

VINCE BELL comes from the same Texas songwriting school that spawned Guy Clark and Townes Van Zandt, and later Nanci Griffith (who covered Bell's "Woman of the Phoenix") and Lyle Lovett (who provides vocal support on this debut). After a near-fatal encounter with a drunk driver, Bell has returned with the album of a lifetime in *Phoenix*. The music has an unsettling quality, as the everyday details in his songs never quite resolve the mystery at their heart. The spare arrangements are spellbinding, with producer Bob Neuwirth recruiting guitarists Geoff Muldaur and Stephen Bruton, violinist David Mansfield, pianist John Cale, harmonica whiz Mickey Raphael, and vocalist Victoria Williams for this labor of love.

MUSICIAN MAGAZINE

VINCE BELL Texas singer/songwriter Vince Bell has come back from the dead to see his debut record issued on the Austin-based Watermelon label...

Phoenix is a record of [his] struggle. Produced by Bob Neuwirth, and featuring a cast of musicians that include Victoria Williams, Lyle Lovett, John Cale, Steve Bruton, and Mickey Raphael, the disc is a haunting, spare set of recollections that recall Robert Johnson in their stark intensity and Hank Williams in the country simplicity. "I was thinking to myself who could have come back and done this. I couldn't come up with anybody," Bell says.

♪ XXXII ♪

The Poetry in the Prose

T. Bone Burnett wrote the liner notes to *Phoenix*:

> Vince Bell, is, as far as I know, the only writer who has ever read his own obituary. In between Indio and Joshua Tree his tape turns around for about the fifth time. It is other worldly music. Heart breaking music. In a world of entertainment and musick—a world that celebrates the sameness of all things— this is music that celebrates the differences. Magical unrealism. Poetry from the solitary world of rank strangers—savaged into a state of grace...
>
> Just past Joshua Tree there's a bumper sticker on a bent up '74 Dodge pickup that claims Jesus will be back soon. I hope that's true. But in the meantime, happily, Vince Bell is back now.

I had begun preparing for the aftermath of this album a long time ago, and from the bottom of the barrel, in the deafening quiet of Music School. Today, I was exactly where I had craved to be during that dark, trackless time. Now I had the same problems everyone else had. Be careful what you wish for.

Bob Neuwirth may have said it best: "So you wanted to be an artist. Now you are. Live with it." And if the living wasn't as easy as I had imagined, at least I was pushing the envelope again, and on my own.

Before I left that bucolic little tourist town of Fredericksburg three years later, I bought a used computer, divorced my independent record label, got turned down for jury duty, played at The Bottom Line in New York, couldn't book enough gigs, got world-class reviews, and penciled another album or two's worth of tunes. I was relentlessly at it every day. But earning the title "Legendary" doesn't necessarily pay all the bills.

I also wrote a book about my decade of recovery; that book would eventually become part of this one. For the first time, I relied on the spirit of the prose alone to express my thoughts. I had never intended to write prose. Because of the powerful impressions made on me by people like Lennon, I had regarded prose as an arcane art form.

I had started writing about the aftermath of my accident in Berkeley but had exhausted myself writing 30 pages, saying, "That's it. That's the story." Right. So I got back up on that carousel pony in the quiet little Central Texas town and wrote the other couple of hundred pages: Two hundred and four pages in 184 days.

My favorite room of the big, turn-of-the century house we lived in was the limestone front porch shaded by a huge hackberry tree. It was framed by white wooden gingerbread against a yellow background with a heavy, dark-green swing to one side where one could escape for unrehearsed moments.

From that swing, I could look out across the widest streets in Texas. The block was made up of rough-hewn, 150-year-old mortared stone-and-timber houses beneath stands of pecan, the ubiquitous hackberry, and live oak trees. The roads in my little town were originally constructed broadly so that wagon teams could turn around in them.

The town was so small that everyone knew everyone. Down at the grocery, I offered to let the kindly German local and her bag of ham hocks go ahead of me and my bottle of wine. When my turn came, I instinctively produced a driver's license with my check as if I was ordering a beer on Venice Beach. The nice young lady at the register said, rather dismissively for an otherwise polite Hill Country native, "We know where to find you," as she handed my license back. Now, that's a small town in Texas.

As our typical day at home went along, I ducked back out the front door to worry the latest tune or just get away from the computer for a blessed moment. I swung gently back and forth with the ever-present cup of coffee in my hand. From there, I did some of my hardest thinking. In my head, I went over signature licks and chord passages to music I hadn't even played yet. I appreciated anything that helped as I confronted the elusive authorship process that never hints of itself more than it has to. The vision of my dreams from the peeling old porch was clearer than my sight.

At the closing of yet another productive day on the "box" computer for Sarah, and the "box" guitar for me, the heat ebbed into the coming evening. We enjoyed a glass of white wine together over some end-of-day conversation. Tomorrow we'd take on the world again where we left off tonight, poetry close and yet continents away from the limestone front porch and that old green swing.

> From a letter to Peter Blackstock:
> Wasn't trying to be difficult yesterday about the kind of music I play. No, as I explained, I've been playing to please since I was marveling at the sheet music in my mother's piano bench. It seems plain to me, but here now, many songs into my writing career with my dear old six-string, there's more

music in me than any traditional style has to offer. Others sometimes prefer the description "quirky." I know it for what it is . . .

. . . above the ecliptic.

From a letter to my grandmother:

So, from the green porch swing in little Fredericksburg I'm going to play guitar in Greenwich Village in Manhattan. Anybody who is anybody has performed there sometime in his career. Maybe that means a review. Everyone at my house hopes so.

On the home front, I played my first back-to-back dates in over 12 years. I got treated like royalty on a dirt road outside San Antonio, and in New Braunfels. It sure has been rough from not being able to walk, or talk.

My break-playing friend, Bill Browder, said, "Boy, you must have practiced a lot lately to sound so together." I reassured my long-time pal he couldn't . . .

. . . see that far.

♪ *XXXIII* ♪

Play Like You Practice

I took three trips to Europe during that Texas stay. The first was in 1995 to Holland and Belgium as the supporting act for the Jayhawks.

March 22 Tivoli, Utrecht (w/The Jayhawks)
        23 Paradiso, Amsterdam (w/The Jayhawks)
        24 Luna, Brussels, Belgium
        25 Noorderlicht, Tilburg (w/The Jayhawks)
        26 Leidsekade Live (National Radio Show) (afternoon)
              Nighttown, Rotterdam (w/The Jayhawks) (evening)
        27 Oosterpoort, Gronlingen (w/The Jayhawks)
        28 Zalen Schaaf, Leeuwarden (w/The Jayhawks)
        30 Tom Tom Club, Heythuizen
        31 Cactus Club, Brugge, Belgium

When I did my own solo dates as well, Sarah, our driver Bert, and I saw the kilometers in between. In Den Bosch, it was at a joint down from a twelfth-century cathedral and a Mexican restaurant. Utrecht was a busy, paved-over university town, and a whistle-stop on the rail line between Amsterdam and Rotterdam. On the border with Belgium, I played the hippest spot in a little hamlet. There weren't as many people walking the one street in the day as there were for my show that night. In Brussels, the guitar and I did a TV show in the morning and a horse-barn-turned-bar that evening.

> From a letter to my father:
> Wow! What a trip. We stayed mostly in Amsterdam down the street from the Van Gogh and the Rijksmuseum. We'd travel each day to another part of the country, or to Belgium to do interviews, or to perform on TV shows, radio shows, and in concert halls. Our drivers were tops, and everyone spoke English. Other than us packing a little too much, I'm not sure anything went wrong on this trip, thanks to them.
> Bert Van de Kamp, the most influential and gracious reviewer in Holland, said, "His guitar is so big, and his voice is so big. These large stages swallow solo songwriters, but not Vince."

I looked out to a standing-room-only crowd at the Paradiso off the Leidseplein in Amsterdam. This joint may well be the top place for a musician to play on this planet. Pink Floyd has played here, Prince has played here. It was filled to overflowing by the Jayhawks and me. There were no chairs.

My tuner was on the stool next to me, geigering in red and green LED spikes to the notes I quietly played. I had been practicing or performing for decades. I knew the chords, and I knew the melodies by heart. I'd forgotten more jokes than you'd ever heard, and I was ready for another. I was pumped. The promoter introduced me as I banged out some opening chords on the "cannon." Everything seemed to be working just as I'd planned as I rifled into the first number. Except one thing. I couldn't hear a nickel of the vocal I had rehearsed for weeks. All the speakers, amps and cords, mics, risers, and lights, and I couldn't hear a word of what I'm saying to 1,500 Dutch people and the fellow who books the Rolling Stones.

The monitor mix was a mystery. The sound of my guitar was disappointingly unfamiliar. The old dreadnought's EQ was brittle, overbearing, and unforgiving. There was no bottom end to the instrument. It made the passing chords to my songs sound ignorant. It made the way I play sound ignorant. It was way too loud. By comparison, my vocal was dull and puny despite stage monitors up to my knees. As I wrote in the Black Book, IF YOU CAN'T BE COOL, YOU CAN'T STAND . . . ON ONE LEG. You'd have thought that doing lyric passages would be difficult. But, guess what? I'd memorized the words.

In that situation, I don't know how anyone else does it, but I play the way I practiced. Even when I can't hear a note of what I'm doing live and in person. Nothing like a show by rote with no ears. It's almost as if I can judge an unheard note from the vibrations in my head.

The booking agent for the Stones left for the party tray backstage in the middle of the first song. Trying to keep it together, I caught someone's eye in the front row at the start of the second tune and smiled at them like I'd been reading their mail.

I took a second trip to Europe with several other solo players—Iain Mathews, David Olney, and Eric Taylor. We did a songwriter-in-the-round for 18 dates in 21 days. Austria, Switzerland, Germany, Belgium, and the Netherlands flew by the windows of the van that carried us all. Hamburg was the most comfortable gig, Berlin was impressive with all the diversity and those wide, Texas-size boulevards. We did radio shows from Potsdam, and in Holland on a sidetracked train car that had been owned by some orgiastic Eastern European despot. After the endless hard work to relearn an hour set, playing one song and then watching three or four songs by other performers trail by seemed strange. It just ain't the way we trained.

The third time I woke on a Boeing 747 after a full night of travel, I turned 45 years old 37,000 feet over the Atlantic Ocean. I was on my way to a record company festival in Utrecht, the Netherlands, that featured two stages and 14 American acts.

I groggily made my way through customs and collected my effects from the rotating luggage belt. After a short wait, I became awfully sure that the driver sent to meet me was not going to show up. I negotiated a currency exchange and the coin-operated phone, and called my guitar-playing accompanist, none other than David Rodriguez, my old barrister friend, now living in the Netherlands. When he answered, I was swimming in the silent water-ballet of intercontinental travel. "David, good to hear a familiar voice. I don't think the driver from the concert is going to pick me up."

He asked, "Do you have 50 guilders?"

"Yes," I replied.

"Well, get a cab. We'll be here waiting for you."

We began a rehearsal schedule that consumed a few hours of the next three days. When we weren't rehearsing, we walked through Amsterdam past places like the Museum of the Tropics, roved through the metro station full of shops, or went to the Cafe de Omval across the canal from David's flat.

On Friday, I met my piano player for the Sunday concert, Jur Scherpenziel. He ran a blues bar in Amsterdam and our final rehearsal was held on his stage. The walls were festooned with rockabilly posters and pictures of famous customers. He had a ready smile and a slow, confident demeanor that made him seem trustworthy from the onset. Sometimes, players are eccentric to the point of being more trouble than they are worth, but this accompanist was a comfort. A small cigar hung casually from his mouth. My voice was hoarse after several hours. I was glad that it was the last day of rehearsal.

Saturday dawned with rehearsal mercilessly over. I loved being a quarter of the way around the planet in pursuit of music, but the break was more than welcome. My driver was supposed to arrive at

6:30 that evening to take me to Utrecht and the hotel near the concert site. By 8:30, she hadn't arrived; but this is the same driver who had missed picking me up at the airport days before, so I knew she must be close.

By 9:00, I was flying toward Utrecht in a van with crusty-looking, half-dazed band members of another group in the farthest backseat. As the driver wound dizzily around the town in no recognizable pattern, they moaned with a familiar air of futility: "You're not going to end up back at the airport again, are you?" She assured them that we were, really, on the way to Utrecht now.

On Sunday I walked over for a sound check in the immense facility where the show would be held. It had several presentation halls. The largest, the site of my concert, was heavily wood-grained with steep seats around a spacious stage. The big hall was cluttered with Anvil cases full of sound equipment higher than my head.

The rationale around a sound check is ostensibly to set the levels of your presentation appropriately and precisely. What the engineers don't tell you is that the quality of sound changes radically when any surface that tones bounce off of is altered. Imagine what happens to the frequency characteristics of an auditorium filled with warm, undulating bodies. The upshot is that the better part of the hour you invest in sound-checking is tossed to the breeze when the first 20 people amble through the front door. And the time you spend waiting around for your vocal and guitar check is only exceeded by the time spent watching someone else string cords and plug in speaker boxes as stage crews set up microphones and check monitors.

Afterwards, when I opened my dressing-room door, there sat a nine-foot-long grand piano with Jur at the keyboard, practicing passages from the songs for the show. David was sitting next to him, guitar at the ready, helping him chart some bars that missed scrutiny in rehearsal. I closed the door. Sound emanating from the stage area was muffled now. People were anxiously running back and forth in various states of record-company frenzy.

The hardest thing about playing to a crowd has nothing to do with standing up in front of a bank of blinding lights or remembering how to execute the most complex music. Instead, it revolves around the anonymous moments before the show, which seem to last forever until things get moving faster than you can keep track. It's during this time that you remember you forgot to turn off the coffee machine.

Finally the time arrived for the first set of music we had ever played together, anywhere. As we were introduced, I looked around to see if I had my guitar and cords. The picks were on my fingers alright and the capo was in the clip of my strap. The other players stood by me in the wings as the host finished a long-winded introduction.

We emerged on a spotlight-covered corner of stage left. With guitars, bass, and drumsticks in hand, we trotted to our respective places underneath the fanfare of lights sweeping the dark, spacious area. I automatically began the first few bars of Gary Burgess's "Frankenstein." Forty minutes later, we pulled off an energetic version of "Hard Road" to conclude the set and trotted back offstage to the sound of enthusiastic Dutch applause.

Five thousand miles of air travel. Six days of rehearsal. Live and in person for only two-thirds of an hour. I relaxed after the show, talking casually to friends and reviewers.

The next morning, the same cheerfully late driver arrived, roughly on time, outside the Hotel Smits with another band already loaded. I climbed into the captain's seat across from her and listened to the jokes the others told. In an hour we were back at Shiphol International Airport. After the baggage and ticket check-in, we players began milling around the terminal. In our private thoughts, we all looked forward to getting home. With eleven hours in the air over the Atlantic yet again and another search of my belongings at customs ahead, I kept to myself.

Thoughtfully tapping a rolled magazine on my thigh, with a steaming cup of coffee in my other hand and the companion black bag over my shoulder, I stood at the full-length windows in one of the promenades. I gazed at the busy runways and airliner approaches. The raucous noise of jet engines, baggage tractors, and shouting men contrasted with a pastoral, seventeenth-century cathedral in the distance. When I took off my sunglasses, closed my eyes, and gently rubbed them, they burned. I was so tired, my temples ached, as I slipped into the twilight of another transatlantic voyage.

Between the last of those two European trips I gave a speech and played a few songs at the Texas Brain Injury Association Conference in Austin. After all the guitar and I had gone through to reunite with one another and with the message inside the music, it was a thrill to perform for over a thousand people and tell them our story. My genuine hope was that perhaps some poor other injured body could figure it all out as I had. If I could make a normal world for my guitar and me to live in again, maybe they could too.

> From a letter to a brain injury survivor about performing poetry:
> The performance sounds great. The more the better, and the faster you will learn the art form. It's the only way to get good at presentation.
> All the rehearsal I do here at Music School doesn't amount to much when I get on any stage whatsoever. It has its own list of qualities to be figured. In other words, after you have written the poetry just so, then you have to deal with the moments in between. That way the spaces between the notes or words become as influential as the notes or words themselves.
> You have to be able to get from the end of one song to the start of another, and you'll find some of the more creative things you will pull off in a night are not programmed. So you have to become fluent in "off the cuff." Here you will surprise

yourself and discover some of the thrill of the chase. As in chasing encores, which is what performance is all about.

Don't get me wrong, the one doesn't happen without the other, but being onstage after a good rehearsal schedule is a "technique" that must be found, just as surely as the basic text you labor over at the anonymity of your desk.

Three years after we moved back to Texas with a backseat full of cats, we departed from the rangy peach groves and the sprawling goat farms of that parched part of the world for Tennessee, this time with three cats and a dog in the back.

We moved to a cabin across a two-lane road from a produce stand in the hardwoods. It was just off the Hundred Highway: Tennessee 100. And I mean 20 or 30 feet off the highway. We lived just out of earshot of a mélange of metropolitan Nashville weed-eaters, leaf-blowers, bug lights, and lawnmowers.

♪ *XXXIV* ♪

Texas Plates

*T*wo months after moving to Nashville, we packed up the Jeep with the guitar, the border collie, and boxes of CDs and made a swing through the northwestern U.S., playing not only in Washington and Oregon but also Montana, Colorado, New Mexico, and Texas. In Portland, it was NXNW, the Pacific Northwest's version of Austin's SXSW. In Denver, it was a show with Bill Morrissey, during the worst snowstorm they'd seen that early in the year in decades.

Finally settled in the hollow in the Nashville woods, I began to record my second CD, *Texas Plates*, with producer Robin Eaton. Just as with *Phoenix*, the basics were recorded live: me and my guitar, Mickey Grimm on drums, percussion, and cajon. Over the next year outstanding players were added: Pat Bergeson, Lewis Brown, Pat Buchanon, Chris Carmichael, Dave Jacques, Brad Jones, Al Perkins, Ross Rice, Aly Sujo. Kami Lyle, and Maura O'Connell sang harmonies. I thought it ironic that Maura, a woman from Ireland, sang some of the more ringing notes on "Second Street," to help me typify what, a half a world away, is in the hearts of a truckload of Tejanos as we were all looking for work.

The new album got its name when I turned around a year or so after I'd moved to Nashville and realized I still had Texas license plates on the Jeep. An old drummer of mine, Jim Alderman, had moved to Nashville from Texas four years earlier. His wife hadn't let him change their license plates.

I took a tip from a publisher friend and found a place for my CD on an affiliate of a major record label. When I asked an L.A. companion with vast experience in the record industry if I should chance it with one of the dastardly majors, he replied, "Everyone except Michael Jackson and Madonna has been fired from a major label, so go get fired."

While I was waiting for the release of the new CD, I began the mother of all podcasts, six years before there was such a word. I started recording and broadcasting my music on a $135 computer that my sister Shary had given me. The 1.01 program I used, and the files it created, were readable by the computer programs that were available in all the major studios. Whatever I did could be edited, added to, or altered as if I had recorded it in one of the high-dollar labs.

With such cheap technology, I embarked on a 28-week series broadcast from my new website, vincebell.com, and called it "Live Music's Cool at Live Music School." No cover charge, no drink minimum. I ran upwards of a hundred tunes from all eras of my authorship, with accompaniment on percussion and accordion by Jim Alderman. Renditions of songs from *Texas Plates*, *Phoenix*, and the *Complete Works of Vince Bell* were featured. I even ran the "Riverside recording," the three songs I had been doing in the studio on December 21, 1982.

Thanks to yet another used computer hooked up to the Internet in the other room and garrisoned by Sarah, I appeared on radio programs across the globe without leaving my back room. Early on, Internet radio interviews from Florida, England, and the Netherlands highlighted the effort. I always thought it odd that I came to Nashville to shuck and jive the intransigent music business, only to discover a wellspring of artistic freedom from the computer on my desk.

> From a letter to Jim Musser:
> Yo. This is Vince.
> I'm going to start putting live recordings on my website. They have come from a microphone I set up at my desk. My voice and guitar, but nothing less than CD quality. I bet it will be better than the sound at 99% of the grab 'em, stab 'em bars I've outlived over many a year now.
> Like the basics to *Texas Plates*, which were recorded in 30 hours on the 28 and Mickey Grimm's wooden box (called the cajon), an old drummer of mine from Tejas came in and bashed and slashed on a collection of widgets he found in his garage.
> This idea reminds me of the kid who craned to listen to the AM radio in his mother's fire-engine-red Mercury Monterey convertible in the late '60s and '70s. Back then, you didn't give a rat's ass about sound quality, you only cared if the Zombies or the Kinks were on the play list.
> Oh, and about the 30 hours? I slept the middle 10.
> vince

Texas Plates was in stores on April 13, 1999. The release party saw me onstage at Nashville's Exit/In. Robin Eaton played bass, Mickey Grimm percussion, and Kami Lyle sang harmony. After all the spirit that had gone into making that CD, I'd like to remember it as a special night, but frankly it was a major label letdown.: an event that meant more to the people who had nothing to do with making the art than to those of us who had.

A month or so later, I received a plaque from the mayor of the City of Austin for my early book on my decade of recovery. It was a Chairman's Commendation from the Austin Mayor's Committee for People with Disabilities. That was flattering, but I needed to work, as usual, in the worst way. I began to feel out the scene at the bars and studios in Nashville. A quick canvas of the nightlife convinced me I hadn't much of a reason to compete with my fellow players for the dearth of jobs available. I met a bunch of them and found every one of them had put just as much hard work into his art as I had. It was time to hit the road.

> From a letter:
> I flew into Toronto, Canada, and played with Stephen Fearing in Port Dover on the north shore of Lake Erie. It was yet another real privilege. Our concert was held in a classic old vaudeville-style theatre on the main street of that little beach town. My foray into North Texas a couple of hundred kilometers east of Detroit was charmed.
> Like I told them at a later date from the stage at the Corner Coffeehouse in New Market, Ontario:
> "Hell, you people are almost in Oklahoma."

As the sun disappeared, the breeze picked up, and people began to arrive for the evening's festivities. Stephen and I wandered around the dressing room with guitars around our necks, mumbling lyrics and faking guitar parts. There were mirrors on the walls reflecting every move we made in triplicate, but it was also as if neither one of us was really there. A stagehand stuck his head up out of the brick stairwell going down to the auditorium, "Five minutes, Vince?"

"Yeah, yeah, yeah," I replied offhandedly.

Stephen paused in an air guitar passage, "Ride 'em, cowboy."

I disappeared into that stairwell. At the bottom, it was pitch black except for a pale blue light onstage. A Flying Burrito Brothers CD filled the room while I stumbled into curtains. The monitor man with a penlight and I introduced ourselves and shook hands as the crowd growled to itself like a den of sleepy lions. "Don't you get a little nervous when you do this?" he asked.

Like a big cat I yawned, "It's a little late for that, don't you think?"

✦ ✦ ✦

Another early promo tour for "the *Plates*" landed me on an eight-seat twin engine that taxied like an insect to a runway ten times its size at Washington Dulles. Years ago, the one-terminal airport used to rumble like a subway station when a jet landed. This time, I was just passing through one of the new, outer terminals to play radio in Charleston, West Virginia, at *the* live radio program in America, *Mountain Stage*.

I had spent what seemed like a year in Texas the week before playing in Dallas, Galveston, Houston, and Austin. Then I drove home with Sarah a thousand miles to gig in Nashville till one in the morning, and didn't sleep before I boarded a plane for Charleston the next day.

The pilots left the door open to the cockpit on the flight, and I sat just behind them looking out the front windows. One hour later, from 14,000 feet, we descended to Charleston. One of the hosts and a pretty, young driver met me at the gate. We all instinctively angled for the baggage carousel a floor away. Through all the polite conversation no sleep will afford, I was lucky to be standing. It was good to have sunglasses.

As the same bags passed in front of us several times, I approached a baggage attendant to find that neither my clothes nor my guitar had ever left DC. And that I might not see them 'til after the show half a day from then. I was so fried by lack of rest I had to laugh. Turning to my resourceful host, I said, "You got a guitar?"

He said, "Sure."

"Let's go to the show."

Mountain Stage is taped in a large theatre on the West Virginia capitol grounds. I offered to the packed audience, "These people have my underwear, folks."

The four songs I performed sounded great. Everything ran smoothly, and I met some new buddies including Dougie MacLean;

Tony Bowles, the guitarist for the Amazing Rhythm Aces; and the excellent *Mountain Stage* house band.

The next morning, anticipating the next show's lineup of acts milling about, I left this note stapled to the wall backstage:

> Yo, you're in the Green Room.
>
> My name is Vince Bell. I'm just a poor finger-picker from Tejas and this is a true story.
>
> Firstly, I didn't even have a change of clothes before I played. I arrived in sunglasses, a pair of sweats, and a T-shirt. No one held it against me, not even the house band. The glib fellows said, "So what, this is radio."
>
> Secondly, I didn't have a guitar when I showed up, either. But those excellent musicians in the house band strapped some strings around my neck, and pointed me at the microphone and a packed theater. After the show I went to the hotel room. There sat my 28, bigger than life in the flight case. It could have had a pretty little blue bow on it, but I didn't care.
>
> Lastly, I did not sleep the night before my show, thanks to some bar in Nashville.
>
> Have a great show yourself. Since this radio show I've been resting like Elvis. He's still dead. I'm playing smooth like Dougie MacLean. He's great.
>
> And these days I got more clothes than Mao.

♪ *XXXV* ♪

Say in Your Owndamnway

Sometimes the loudest sound in my cabin outside of Nashville was the rice frying. When songs are trying to become songs, it's quiet as death, hour in and hour out, except for cursing punctuations in the midst of the music I envision. Write, and rewrite, and rewrite, and rewrite. Sometimes till you've made a huge circle of scrabbling in the sky, only to find you've come out the other side facing the original. It's the worst of the work. It's no wonder the frets on a guitar get ruts in them as fast as they do. Over and over, round and about, up and down, and back again. Poor damn guitar.

Then, what you faithfully scrawl you must, discouragingly, learn. And it never goes as easy as you might suppose it would. You can write songs for 30 years, but your hard-won latest always turns out to be just different enough from the rest to qualify as a whole new sonorous complication.

Ambition sure is lonely.

I was very high on *Texas Plates*. But the hulking Godzilla of an entertainment label was no more impressive in its efforts to market my presentation than the independent from Austin that had buried my first. In my Black Book I wrote:

MUSIC ROW
Those pencil dicks
almost made me frightened
to be who I was.

December found us driving a few thousand miles doing dates in the eastern U.S., and all the while I was working on a song. It began clumsily, but confidently enough, at my desk back in Tennessee. On the interstate in Connecticut, it shed its confidence and its refrain. Oh, well. In Andy Revkin's guestroom on the Hudson just outside of Cold Spring, more of the early musings became woefully obsolete and were summarily jettisoned.

After we broke down in Torrington, Connecticut, a few days later, Sarah and I ended up at Tom Pacheco's in Woodstock, New York. He and I traded stories and songs at the kitchen table. We lasted for hours. It had been a helluva long time since we had seen each other, and since I'd scrawled his name on my yellow pad at Brackenridge.

When our traveling circus split the next day, I started in again on the piece, with my thesaurus, my rhyming dictionary, and my notebook arranged around me in the front seat of the Jeep. We took the thruway west. I rarely looked up. The next stop was Syracuse, where the Midwest begins, said Pete Seeger.

Finally our route led down to the borough of Manhattan. There, with gigs completed and after Christmas with relatives and friends new and old, my hard work began to pay off. You have to have the patience of the ages to follow up on these three-minute wonders. A whole eraser or two later, my little glimmer of an idea that hardly resembled its original self started perking right up. As I completed the last of the verse, the irony of finishing a piece about courage and conviction on the barren, rocky plains of Central Texas while I was 20 floors above civilization in New York City was not lost on me.

It was New Year's Eve. And many of them I had seen from a stage, but on this particular one I put the music away for the night. On the 86th-floor observation deck of the Empire State Building, just after sunset, flash cubes of the tourists were going off like flares. Gazing back down into my glass, I was finally satisfied with my effort, and glad it was over after 3,000 miles of edits.

100 MILES FROM MEXICO

A hundred miles from Mexico,
me and my amigo, the coral orange moon.
Dark so black poets don't go.
Ol' fateful, willin' who I am
on a fateful, winding stretch of road

One hundred miles from Mexico,
the moon, the music, and me.

A hundred miles from Mexico,
backing down this highway,
thumbing at the headlights.
Gravel shoulder, Devil's backbone.

Before the headlights become the dawn
me and my amigo will be gone.

When I returned to the 100 Highway in Nashville, I left the bars to them that could, or would, and changed my focus to recording another CD. My thoughts were, if I lost the thrills and chills of Saturday night, could I live with that? No sweat. But if I lost the ability to speak my mind with the music that had taught me one helluva lot about this life and how I could live it, that would be a big problem. By now my identity was fully wrapped up in the work of expression. It steeled me with the courage of optimism.

It was always easy to face back down into the tunnel vision of writing. The blinders of penmanship were curious. They made the narrow path I took pursuing the elixir of the inquisitive in a forest of pocket-knife-sharpened pencils a little more reassuring. I never looked back. I was too scared.

And I had never written for an existing market, but instead because it was true. I didn't give a rat's ass whether my words, or my musical notes, were marketable like a trendy hairstyle or a pair of designer jeans. I lived my impractical, often complicated, life to be meaningful. No shortcuts. It wasn't a payback for all the hard work to become someone else's idea of palatable. The payback for all the trouble was to develop the skill and have the conviction to say what you wanted to say in your owndamnway.

I'd get up with a cup of coffee and start recording new songs on the computer. Or typing lyrics that moved me into the yearly update files I had kept since Berkeley. Those constantly updated files in a word processor helped glimmers of perspective come from under my hat.

Sometimes the music is first, sometimes the lyrics. That it works at all is the magic. From way before those soggy days living in Montrose into whatever tomorrow brings, I have always been, and will probably always be, a composing lyricist strapped to an orchestra that, in a beer light, looks suspiciously like an acoustic guitar.

There certainly have been the doubters about the worlds I created. And others I would have judged more than capable of accepting my uncompromising perspective with the imaginative art form just never . . . did . . . get it.

In another new wrinkle, I had tuned my guitar down a whole step, like a baritone guitar minus the scale, for *Texas Plates*. And it worked. My voice, powered by a still partially paralyzed vocal cord from that auto crash, was better accommodated at the lower pitch. When people were curious, "Nice guitar, but how did you get that expressive, smoky voice?"

Dry like leftover toast, "Really, you don't want to know."

Now I could work the lyric passage to my pieces with much greater control. My self-devised pick style, coupled with an easier action, were made for each other. The lower part of my vocal range that it called for was better. It put me two baby steps toward singing with a new guitar style.

♪ *XXXVI* ♪

The Bottom Line

I was asking for an adventure, and I got it. Six days and five nights on a bus, 118 Americano dollars, Nashville to New York. And back. Forty straight hours of bumping up and down, with 47 other completely miserable people in spaces smaller than coffins stacked next to one another, with a chemical toilet at the left rear back.

I got on at the Nashville Greyhound station at two o'clock in the afternoon on a Monday. I was truly was sad about Sarah not coming along. Very hard to say goodbye. But, let the dance begin. I was going to New York to play with Lyle Lovett in the Village for his album release. He had recorded a CD of Texas writers who had influenced his music, *Step Inside This House*. Including my song "I've Had Enough" was a cherishable and flattering tribute. He was playing at the Bottom Line for two nights. My night included Lyle, Willis Alan Ramsey, Guy Clark, and me. Good enough.

We had tried to make a reservation for the plane three weeks in advance, but that was going to cost a thousand bucks. Later efforts got that down to about 600. The "dog" was only $118. I was a writer and a player trying to get a book and a CD out at the same time, and Sarah and I need every cent. It was worth it.

Crossville, Knoxville, Johnson City, Bristol, Abingdon, Wyethville, Marion (a prison ringed in zipper wire across the road from the bus depot), Roanoke, Harrisonburg, D.C., New York. Twenty hours. No stop over 30 minutes, but a stop every hour, somewhere. Fog, and rain, glaring dusk, truck-stop sandwiches, headlights in black-as-pitch, morning before the sun in places with no name that look like all the other places with no name in the haze of almost lunch. At the Port Authority, under cloud cover, I put my wallet in my front pocket.

It was a three-buck cab fee to the swank hotel on 51st up from Times Square that my compadre Wayne Lawrence had gotten for us. The tip was as large as the fare. Wayne and I had pizza on 42nd while President Clinton was across the street at a Broadway play. The limos outside gleamed and were as long as cigars. The neighborhood was covered with men in gray suits, with tiny ear jacks that disappeared into their coats. When we passed a group of them, it was as if we weren't even there. Thank goodness for small favors.

Next day I talked on phones, missed appointments, and saw an editor for the *New York Times: Sunday Magazine* in a Brazilian restaurant. I told him, "The Internet is where I'll market my new CD and my book." I suited out for the gig, the limo Wayne had ordered showed up late, but time has compressed and we warped through an asteroid belt of traffic down Broadway. Wayne dressed and undressed the driver for the delay, a brilliant, no-nonsense deadpan that measured with the best of them.

Surprise of surprises: Steven Fromholz was there. I was going to have a good time. We met backstage and fell in love again. The night began with all five of us onstage together. We traded songs for two and a half hours and did a second show at 11 o'clock.

When all was said and done, we sang our way through two shows of full houses. We all got laughs, we all knew the punch lines to everyone else's jokes. If I'd had a nickel for every note I'd known by heart, I could have bought Manhattan. That's knowing four other guys and their work a lot of years. We were all visibly pleased with one another and happy to be together in a Village club in the big town. We played a dozen songs apiece in the two shows and nothing much over again. There were movie stars lurking about, there was cigar-smoking, and we toasted everything.

Sarah had gotten word of the show back home on the Internet. An hour after we'd finished she knew more about it than I did.

I was back at the Port Authority early the next day, and I sat on my guitar case just outside the door, street side up a flight of stairs from the avenue. New York is a terrifically noisy town. I pulled out the cell phone, fired up a smoke, and called Sarah to find out how I had done the night before. The reviews were flattering; it felt good to have wagered so much with so little.

By 6:00 that evening, I didn't think about the show anymore. I was back on the bus and headed for Washington, D.C. I rolled up my sweatshirt and stuck it under my head and closed my eyes. This "express" bus stopped more places than the one coming up had. I lost my window seat talking on the cell phone till it ran out of charge, and almost missed the re-boarding.

Sarah was waiting for me at the bus station when I arrived home in Nashville and drove me out of my daze of 40 hours of bus travel in five days. It took 48 hours to return to somewhat normal.

Just a few months later, I hopped an SUV for Tejas with a couple of high-mileage, low-maintenance friends from Chicago for another performance with Lyle and the other artists whose songs he had recorded on his recent CD, this time on *Austin City Limits*.

The drive from Nashville to Austin was 900 miles. In one jump. About 11 hours after we began in Cowboytown, we ended up at a friend's house behind a cafe on Lake Austin Boulevard.

The following day's regimen included rehearsal at one of Austin's larger clubs in order to accommodate all the writers and the band. After I arrived and found a comfortable place to lay my things out, off to the side of the large stage area, "Frogboltz" snuck up from behind and did the lip lock on me. With my feet off the floor, I confided to an astonished gathering while chuckling breathlessly in the strong embrace, "... I-it's the hair coloring."

We all sang, and the band played with us all, as if we'd been there for days. Onstage with our guitars around our necks, I spent a few moments showing Lyle the chord changes to "Woman of the Phoenix." Three songs apiece from each songwriter would be edited down to two for the final TV program.

On the morning of the show, I woke up with a thickening tickle in my throat and nose. I felt green, like the penicillin on an orange. And I hadn't eaten for at least a day. But as I explained offhandedly to one my partners, "You know, we players are programmed to ignore this shit." The cold symptoms drifted annoyingly in and out but were held in check thanks to constant vitamins. I finally ate and then caught the shuttle bus from the hotel to the television studio.

The second practice session with the band went without a hitch. While leaning back on my elbows in the bleacher seats before the taping, I looked out to the controlled confusion of the studio set. An electric cherry-picker truck the size of an economy car had a video camera on the end of a telescoping ladder and scuttled about making hardly a sound. Directors arranged camera angles and talked over headphones to stage managers with light meters. Assistants with clipboards rushed in and out of the large room, while crews laid massive cables for sound and lights. We players were either onstage sound-checking or milling around in various states of ready on our way to the makeup room. Then the crowd began to filter in.

I realized something rather extraordinary, relaxing in my dressing room away from the din. I was the only person still playing the same instrument I had when I introduced some of those fellows to one another.

♪ *XXXVII* ♪

Live in Texas

*T*he success of a good piece was its impor-
tance to those who cared to listen in the first place. Nonetheless, writing was pushing the envelope for the adventuresome of us. It was as
much unanticipated discovery as it was knowing calculation. Thus the
attraction for someone with a leaky ballpoint pen in a shirt pocket and
nothing but a table napkin, or a matchbook cover, on which to illustrate
before the ink runs out. I counted on discerning others to find their
own truths in the scenarios I created. My work was designed to provoke
your thinking, not tell you what to think. But I confess, when a listener
followed the truth that I told, my feet never touched the ground.

Songs were yet a chatty flock in the air above my desk. Sometimes
they'd end up in someone else's hair. At that point they weren't my
problem. If I'd written them well, they'd fly under all sorts of conditions and would return to any handler, experience notwithstanding.

But the writer in me had to push away from the rolltop desk and
turn back into a guitar player again. I could feel the ends of my fingers.
I was out of shape. Back to those awful atonals that put dark green
ruts in the fingers of my left hand.

From a letter to Tom Pacheco:

My stay at your kitchen table at Woodstock a while back has emboldened me. I will record a new album with no help from any label. Just me and the 28. Victoria Williams, the Louisiana woman who sang up *Phoenix* with me, e-mailed, "Welcome to the unhooked generation."

From a letter to Bert Van De Kamp:

I'm putting together an experimental recording this go-round. So there will be a lot more "me" in the final mix, guitar, and vocal. One of the goals of this effort is to produce a credible sound with a minimum of other players so I can tour the end result as it appears on the CD.

Now, with further refinements to my fingerpicking, altering the low tuning of the guitar yet again, and the use of the largest gauge of string I could find, I could play lightly, which is the only way I've ever sounded good anyway. An accented backbeat, inventive new chord forms, and superior sound response that was full and in the front row's face.

A tall Texas friend of mine, Chip Woodburn, deadpanned, "I've baled hay with smaller wire than that."

I was on the road when, out of the blue, I received an e-mail from Vince Pawless, a fine instrument-maker from Dallas. Other pals of mine played his instruments and loved them. His note to me concluded by saying that he wanted to build a guitar for me that I could help design. I flipped. I never anticipated I would have the opportunity to have a guitar designed to accommodate me. A guitar that was built with my desires and style in mind.

ENDORSEMENT
You flatter me somewhat speechless.
As you know from the rough out of my experience . . .
that doesn't happen very often.

From a letter to Vince Pawless:

Vince,

Your offer is fantastic. The opportunity to scheme a guitar with you is pretty dreamy. I thought about it all the way down the interstate playing from Tejas to Tennessee. Tell me when I can contact you at your convenience. I can't wait to see what we might come up with.

Looking forward to it.

Vince

I sent him copies of my CDs to celebrate the effort to build a new kind of guitar from the Southwest, made by Vince, played by Vince.

From a letter to Vince Pawless:

Vince,

Shortly before I recorded my first album, I invented "the claw" in a loft space across the Bay Bridge from San Francisco. It should be pretty obvious to you on these cuts. Maybe this tape will help us design the v2 so that it has that dreadnought characteristic of a great bottom end with the added feature of a strong high-mid like a double-O-series fingerpicking guitar. A brass saddle would help. And the mesquite top might well contribute to these qualities. We'll talk further.

Find me when you will.

v2ince

From a letter to Vince Pawless:

Vince,

Went to the Internet today and looked at some inlay compositions. Full color with pieces of shell. Maybe less is really more, like my music implies.

It's been a pleasure to carry on conversation with you in pursuit of a first-class instrument. I don't see anything similar to this six-string anywhere. It's ahead of the curve. I fully expect it to raise some eyebrows.

It will depict my authorship live and in person as it has developed over the years. Anyone who sees this beautiful guitar

and my face behind it will get the message. My instrument
and I are here to make a difference. Who knows?
>We damn well might.
>v2ince

We communicated back and forth for eight months, sometimes
several times a day, to complete the design part of the project. Because we were both from Texas, I thought we should make a Texas
guitar. And since we both were Vinces, we should call it the v2. For
months, e-mails between VP (him) and v2ince (me) flew back and
forth about all the design parameters imaginable, from the unbent
mesquite pieces for the top and side woods to the gold/ebony tuning
keys of the headstock.

We put a 1935 dreadnought-size neck on a dreadnought box, with
top, back, and sides of mesquite. Mesquite is a rosewood, Texas rosewood. In the bracing inside the guitar and in the neck there are three
or four other exotic woods, zebrawood being one. It has a white-gold
abalone v2 insignia in the sound hole. Bob Sturtevant did the cal-
ligraphy that Vince Pawless in-laid. The nut, saddle, and bridge pins
are made of fossilized mammoth ivory. Those bridge pins had cubic
zirconiums inlaid in their tops. For the v2, the Fossilized Mammoth
Ivory Company in Ft. Worth gave us the first set of fossilized ivory
bridge-pins with cubic zirconiums inlaid in their tops they had ever
made; the second set went to the C. F. Martin Company for their
750,000th guitar. Now, that's Texas.

For the two weeks prior to getting the v2, I was all nerves. I practiced the songs I intended to record for *Live in Texas* on the Martin,
standing in the kitchen with no shirt, no shoes, and a cup of coffee. I
leaned against the sink and performed a set list tacked to the refrigerator door. Sometimes I doubted the decisions about the building of

the v2. I scolded myself, "Someone offered to build you a guitar, and you dreamed up something that looks like a Mexican taxicab."

I bolted at the crack of dawn for four May dates in the Lone Star State. When I arrived 11 hours and 700 miles later in Dallas at Lois and David Byboth's house, the sun was going down. I was on the phone immediately to the other Vince and back out the door for his home on Lewisville Lake.

We shook hands for the first time and he handed me the Vince Bell model Pawless Guitar. A fine instrument. A hardtop dreadnought guitar. My pal, the old dark-top, didn't come out of the case that trip. On this swing, I recorded the CD on the brand new guitar at the Byboths' Texas Nights North house concert. The date ultimately became my third CD, *Live in Texas*. While mixing the recording back in Nashville with my crack engineer, Ely Shaw, we recorded the excellent Cam King on electric guitars that sounded like he had been playing with me at the show. A Bruce Cockburn website called it "a highly recommended private release."

So, after all the designing, what a guitar—unlike any other. The v2 did everything the other guitar did and added its own characteristic sound. And it was well and good to have a new member at Music School in Nashville.

> From a letter to Vince Pawless:
> Vince,
>   After a month or two of playing the v2 back on the Hundred Highway, I saw the old 28 sitting in its stand in the low, slanting glow of sundown pouring through some ancient venetian blinds. It had a crust of dust on it from disuse. I could've written my name on top of those sweat stains.
>   I determined, then and there, something had to be done for my spruce-top pal. I just didn't have what it took to let it sit around and collect the anonymity of that damned dust like some wretched possession fallen out of favor or some curio

in a junk shop. It was always a compatriot. And the thought
of putting it away in the closet just so I could keep owning it
turned my stomach. Squirreling the "cannon" away in some
private darkness or condemning it to display would show a
twisted sense of honor. And I wouldn't be a party to it.

That brave old guitar and I really had to scramble, and we
had laid our ears back and run long and hard. Close as either
one of us ever came to getting away from whatever I was running away from at the time were the words and melodies I
would find on its fret board. To show my infinite commitment to my cherished compadre, I had to let it go.

We each had more songs to tell.

v2ince

♪ *XXXVIII* ♪

Rough Old Texas Hands

I took the Martin to a very hip, very expensive guitar store in Nashville to get it appraised and to find out how the retail world would value my lifelong instrument. The owner appeared when it came out of its flight case the size of a small refrigerator. He said right off the mark that because of its worn, practically varnish-less condition, it probably wasn't worth much. But the last time I performed with that good-for-nothing old bronze, we played for encores. And got 'em.

A grizzled fellow from the excellent repair shop in the back came out especially to see the old campaigner. It was more than an old dog's nose could stand. He smiled warmly but distantly at my well-used pal as if it were his first wife. Then he cooed as he twirled it in the air and remarked all its excellent tolerances. But he matter-of-factly judged, "Other than, obviously, many years of hard livin', it does have a few unglued cracks in the back and sides. And the neck has been sanded down."

Amused at the good fellow's admiration, I said understandingly, "Gentlemen, if you're looking for an original owner, that's me. That ragged old guitar and I have traveled all over this country since I was 19 years old. Now lemme tell ya' both, a piece of sandpaper never came within a light year of it. If the neck is worn, you have no further to look for the reason than my rough old Texas hands."

Six months later, when Vince Pawless came to visit and doctor on the v2 before a swing to New York, I sent him home with my old pal to begin another lifetime of good music. It simply could not have been put in better or more capable hands. My great comfort is that, in going with him, it has never left home.

> From a letter by Vince Pawless:
> v2ince,
>   Visually the 28 expresses its uniqueness in its detail. An old guitar is not as interesting as an old "beat up" guitar. Reason being that "beat up" guitars have more stories. There's enough stories on this guitar as there could be pages in your books.
>   The more I look at this guitar, looking for details or stories, it's filled with 'em. Even on the back edge of the peg head, there are many chips. The Grovers with the plating worn off. The neck with the gloss worn off. The lacquer worn off and replaced by the bare wood from underneath, and not in just the places where it was played, but in the places where it was laid. The Nitrocellulose turning yellow, and then the yellow worn down to the plastic binding to a white. You made this guitar, not the guitar company.
>   vp
> P.S. I think the guitar really belongs to the world, and I just happen to have it in my possession. You know, it's like air, or water.

> And I replied:
> Vince,
>   That guitar will have performed and pleased for over half a century before it's through.
>   And its owner's name will have never changed.
>   v2ince

Index

*Page numbers for poems or song lyrics are in **boldface**.*